T0311703

Cambridge Elements ☰

Elements in Global China
edited by
Ching Kwan Lee
University of California–Los Angeles

CHINA AND GLOBAL FOOD SECURITY

Shaohua Zhan
Nanyang Technological University

CAMBRIDGE
UNIVERSITY PRESS

Shaftesbury Road, Cambridge CB2 8EA, United Kingdom

One Liberty Plaza, 20th Floor, New York, NY 10006, USA

477 Williamstown Road, Port Melbourne, VIC 3207, Australia

314–321, 3rd Floor, Plot 3, Splendor Forum, Jasola District Centre,
New Delhi – 110025, India

103 Penang Road, #05–06/07, Visioncrest Commercial, Singapore 238467

Cambridge University Press is part of Cambridge University Press & Assessment,
a department of the University of Cambridge.

We share the University's mission to contribute to society through the pursuit of
education, learning and research at the highest international levels of excellence.

www.cambridge.org
Information on this title: www.cambridge.org/9781108823814

DOI: 10.1017/9781108914680

First published 2022

A catalogue record for this publication is available from the British Library.

ISBN 978-1-108-82381-4 Paperback
ISSN 2632-7341 (online)
ISSN 2632-7333 (print)

China and Global Food Security

Elements in Global China

DOI: 10.1017/9781108914680
First published online: September 2022

Shaohua Zhan
Nanyang Technological University
Author for correspondence: Shaohua Zhan, shzhan@ntu.edu.sg

Abstract: In less than half a century (1978–2020), China has transformed itself from a country that barely fed itself to a powerful player in the global food system, characterized by massive food imports, active overseas agricultural engagement, and the global expansion of Chinese agribusiness. This Element offers a nuanced analysis of China's global food strategy and its impacts on food security and the international agri-food order. To feed a population of 1.4 billion, China actively seeks overseas agri-food resources whilst maintaining a high level of domestic food production. The strategy gives China an advantageous position in the global food system, but it also creates contradictions and problems within and beyond the country. This could potentially worsen global food insecurity in the long term.

Keywords: China, food security, food system, agri-food order, national–global food duality

ISBNs: 9781108823814 (PB), 9781108914680 (OC)
ISSNs: 2632-7341 (online), 2632-7333 (print)

Contents

1 Introduction

In October 2019, China released a white paper on food security, outlining its food policies whilst also summarizing its achievements on agriculture and food. This was the second time that China released such a report. The first white paper was issued in 1996, in response to the publication of Lester Brown's "Who will feed China?"in 1994 (Brown, 1994). While the two white papers share a common theme in showcasing China's ability to feed its huge population, the contexts of the two reports are rather different. In 1996, China was a country self-sufficient in food. Only 2 percent of staple and feed grain that China consumed were imported, and the country exported more food than it imported. In 2019, however, China had become one of the largest food importers in the world, and a net importer of a variety of food products, including grain, meat, seafood, milk, edible oil, and fruits. The value of food imports to China amounted to US$138 billion in 2019, accounting for 8.8 percent of all food imports in the global market (World Bank, 2021).[1]

The growing food imports to China have revived the question of "who will feed China," stirring up anxiety over the possibility that high food demand in China might lead to global food shortages. During the 2007/2008 food crisis, China's growing food consumption was cited as a contributing factor, even though there was no sudden increase in food imports to the country right before or during the crisis.[2] Lester Brown, the originator of the question, found again a growing interest in his thesis. In 2011 and 2014, he contributed the commentaries titled "Can the United States feed China?" and *Can the World Feed China?*, in which he renewed his analysis of how China's resource constraints, such as water scarcity and farmland loss, and dietary transition would lead to massive food imports to the country and thus starve the world (Brown, 2011, 2014). Brown's doomsday predictions are subject to debate. Some scholars contend that China will be able to increase domestic production to meet most of its food demands. The import of key food commodities to China, such as soybeans, beef, mutton, milk, and sugar, will continue to grow, but the scale of growth will be within the production capacity of the exporting countries (Gong, 2011; Huang, 2013; Huang et al., 2017).

---

[1] The research for this Element is supported by a Singapore Ministry of Education Tier 1 Grant (2020-T1-001-142). According to the data from the World Bank, China still ranked behind the United States in 2019 in terms of the value of food imports; the latter's total food imports amounted to US $159 billion. The US Department of Agriculture, however, ranked China the largest agricultural importer in the world, with an estimated import value of US$133 billion in 2019 (USDA, 2020).
[2] The import of cereals to China declined from 6.3 million tonnes in 2005 to 1.5 million tonnes in 2008, while the import of soybeans had experienced steady growth before and after the food crisis; the volume of soybean imports increased from 27 million tonnes to 37 million tonnes between 2005 and 2008 (National Bureau of Statistics [NBS], 2021a).

There are at least two limitations with the debate over who will feed China. First, both sides focus only on food supply and demand and overlook the very important role of the profit-oriented capitalist agri-food system in affecting food security. The 2007/2008 food crisis, in large part, was not caused by the shortage of global food supply but resulted from the pursuit of higher profits by agribusiness capital, which led to the diversion of resources from food to biofuel production (Chakrabortty, 2008: 7; Bello, 2009). The prediction models of food supply and demand cannot capture the situation of food security without taking into account capitalist dynamics in agricultural and food sectors. In a capitalist system, access to food depends on whether consumers can afford the prices sufficient for capital to maintain profitability. The growing food demand of affluent Chinese consumers has increased profitability of capital in the agri-food sector and stimulated food production in other countries. A decrease in food imports to China, however, may not increase food accessibility for others if capital withdraws from food production due to low profitability. Second, the debate takes the nation-state as the unit of analysis, but food security is a multiscalar phenomenon. To understand the dynamics of the global food system, one should not only examine food production, demand, and trade at the national level but also include global actors such as transnational agribusiness corporations and international organizations. The analysis of subnational actors and dynamics is also necessary. Food security cannot be taken for granted for all social groups, even when the national supply of food is sufficient. The movement of food sovereignty has demonstrated the importance of small food producers in meeting food needs, particularly for those in lower-income brackets (Patel, 2009; Edelman et al., 2014).

The recent literature on China and global food security has started to move beyond the narrow focus of the debate on who will feed China. There have emerged two important strands of research. The first strand focuses on China's overseas agricultural investment, particularly land investment. The earlier studies on this topic, however, suffered by eagerly labelling China as a leading land grabber that threatens food security in the Global South, particularly in Africa (Hofman and Ho, 2012). These studies speculated that China would control large tracts of lands in southern countries and export food products to China regardless of local needs. The problem with these studies was partly due to the politicization of the issue, as media reports and think tanks tended to exaggerate the scale of China's overseas land investment. More recent studies have corrected this bias. It is found that the scale of China's overseas land investment has been grossly overstated. For example, Deborah Bräutigam (2015) revealed that China's land acquisitions in Africa were very limited, far less than what the discourse of a Chinese takeover suggested, and that China exported more food to Africa than it imported from the continent. Recent studies also revealed that China's land deals faced extra scrutiny in host countries and that Chinese investors often had to make significant concessions due to local resistance (Oliveira, 2018; Lu and Schönweger, 2019). Nevertheless, the increasing volume of Chinese overseas agricultural investments suggest that China has adopted a very different food strategy than that in the 1990s: It now not only focuses on domestic production but also is interested in shaping global production and international trade. Furthermore, the issue of land grabbing is important as it reveals the dynamics of global capitalism. The growing literature on land grabbing suggests that global capitalism might have entered a new phase due to the serious constraints on energy and resources, and this will have significant implications for global food security (Borras et al., 2011; McMichael, 2012; Oliveira et al., 2021). Therefore, China's role in the global land rush should be further investigated.

The other strand of research looks at the role of China in reshaping the global food system. This scholarship has been influenced by the literature on the global food regime. Drawing on the world-systems theory and the French regulation school, Harriet Friedmann and Philip McMichael (1989) coined the concept of a global food regime to examine how the international food order had been shaped by world politics and cycles of capital accumulation. The food regime literature focuses on the dynamics of capital accumulation in agri-food sectors, international rules, and formations and transitions of agri-food commodity complexes at and across historical conjectures (Magnan, 2012). Friedmann and McMichael suggest that the global food system has been regulated by successive food regimes. The first regime, in existence from 1870 to 1914 and centered on the British Empire, operated through the colonial extraction of food resources from the periphery in order to feed the European center. The second regime emerged after World War II and was characterized by national agriculture and the food-aid system under US hegemony. There have been debates over whether the global food system has transitioned into a third regime, and if so, how to characterize this third regime (Jakobsen, 2021). Philip McMichael argues that since the 1980s, a corporate food regime has taken hold that subordinates states, producers, and consumers to the interests of corporate capital (McMichael, 2009). Other scholars defined the third regime as "an emergent corporate-environmental food regime" (Friedmann, 2005: 227) or "a neoliberal food regime" (Pechlaner and Otero, 2008: 367). Some scholars disagree on the existence of a third regime, and instead argue that the global food system has been in a period of instability and transition since the breakdown of the second regime in the 1970s (Pritchard, 2009; Belesky and Lawrence, 2019). There are also criticisms of the food regime analysis and the question of whether a global food regime has ever existed (Bernstein, 2016). The debates show that there is no consensus among scholars on whether or how the current global food system has been regulated by a unified food regime. Nevertheless, the literature on a global food regime has highlighted the critical importance of capitalist dynamics, the rise of neoliberal rules and corporate power, and international politics in the global food system.

How will China's increasing food imports and overseas agricultural expansion reshape the global food system?[3] Recent events have elevated the salience of this inquiry. Since 2013, China has been promoting the Belt and Road Initiative (BRI), which aims to build infrastructural and commercial connections between Asia, Europe, and Africa. Although the BRI is not specifically focused on food, it may have significant implications for the global food system as it opens new spaces of agricultural investment and reorganizes agri-food supply chains and trade routes (Tortajada and Zhang, 2021). The trade war and geopolitical rivalry between the United States and China have also signalled the importance of agriculture and food. The agri-food trade has been a key issue in the negotiations between the two countries (Zhang, 2020).

The food regime literature remains ambiguous on the question of whether and how China will transform the global food regime. McMichael (2020) notes that China's agri-food neomercantilism and state capitalism appear to diverge from the free market rules under the corporate food regime, but he is uncertain whether this will lead to the emergence of a new regime. Other observers have noted that China's current involvement in the global food market does not undermine but strengthens corporate power and neoliberal norms (Belesky and Lawrence, 2019). McMichael further draws the analogy between a possible China-centered food system and the first food regime under British hegemony, given that, like the British Empire, China must rely on overseas food resources. He also suggests that the participation of China in the global food market will deepen the East Asian import complex, a phenomenon that emerged during the second food regime but continued to evolve and strengthen in recent decades (Friedmann, 1982; McMichael, 2000, 2020).

This Element critically engages the literature on China and global food security. While addressing the debate over who will feed China and drawing on the studies on China's role in the global food system, the Element distinguishes itself by analytically connecting and integrating China's domestic food dynamics and global food strategy. The main arguments are as follows: China's

---

[3] According to the United Nations (UN), "a food system is defined as a system that embraces all the elements ... and activities that relate to the production, processing, distribution and marketing, preparation and consumption of food and the outputs of these activities, including socio-economic and environmental outcomes" (UN, 2015: 1).

food strategy has gone global, characterized by utilizing food imports to alleviate severe internal resource constraints and by efforts to seek an advantageous position in the global food system, but the success of this global food strategy hinges on whether the country can maintain domestic food supply at a high level. With sufficient domestic supply, China will have leeway to adjust categories and levels of food imports in bargaining with food exporters, and this in turn will enhance its control and utilization of overseas resources. Existing studies often suggest that declining domestic food supply forces China to seek overseas food resources, and that the two constitute a negative correlation – that is, the less food China produces domestically, the more food it will source from overseas. While admitting that the constraints on domestic production is a major factor behind China's global food strategy, this Element argues that the success of China's strategy depends on more, not less, domestic production. I introduce the concept of "national–global food duality" to capture this paradoxical relationship between national food supply and global food strategy. The goal of China's food strategy is to optimize this duality rather than either maximizing food imports or domestic production.

The pursuit of an optimal national–global food duality distinguishes China from the British Empire of the late nineteenth century as well as other East Asian nations in the regional food import complex. Due to their common role as a food importer, McMichael (2020: 120) suggests, "China may emerge as a commanding pole in a food regime of the future, analogous to the British-centered food regime and its re-ordering of an offshore tropical food empire to source (temperate) wage-foods for late-nineteenth century British and European industrial workforces." While China will be a major importer of food, the conditions that underpinned the British-centered food system are absent from China. These conditions were: (1) that European colonial settlements in the New World exploited virgin soil frontiers; (2) that diasporic European farmers and settler states exported farm produce to feed industrial workers in Britain and the European continent; and (3) British hegemony, in which the British Empire exercised both economic and military dominance in the world system (McMichael, 2009). By contrast, China must face an uncertain global food market beyond its control.[4] During the 2007/2008 food crisis, it was domestic production and grain stockpiles that insulated the country from much of the impact. The COVID-19 pandemic had also affected food imports to China in

---

[4] Giovanni Arrighi and Beverly Silver (1999) argued that the unprecedented bifurcation of the leading military power (the United States) and economic power (East Asia, including China) during hegemonic transitions in the capitalist world system would lead to a long period of instability and chaos in global governance. Such instability and chaos will have a strong impact on China's food strategy.

early 2020, and the country again resorted to the harvest of summer wheat and grain stockpiles to ensure sufficient food supply (CCTV, 2020). Thus, different from Britain, China as a food importer has a strong motivation to protect its agriculture and maintain a high level of domestic production.

China's global food strategy will deepen the East Asian import complex, but the country is unlikely to rival other East Asian nations for food-import dependence. The food self-sufficiency rates of Japan, South Korea, and Taiwan (JKT) have all fallen below 40 percent (Lee and Müller, 2012; Niehaus and Walravens, 2017). The East Asian food-import complex emerged during the second food regime, under which the United States dispensed surplus grain to allies and developing countries in the form of food aid (McMichael, 2009: 141). Japan, South Korea, and Taiwan were the US allies and bridgeheads to contain communism. Although they have diversified food-import sources since the 1980s, the geopolitical environment has continued to favor their food-import dependence. Another difference between China and its East Asian neighbors lies in population size. China's population of 1.4 billion is seven times the combined populations of JKT. Were China to follow the East Asian food-dependency model, it must quadruple its already enormous food imports, and this would significantly undermine its bargaining power in the global food system.

This Element does not suggest that a China-centered food regime is emerging on the horizon. This is because China's pursuit of an optimal national–global food duality is less aimed at playing a leadership role in the global food system than at mitigating the risks of a volatile global food market, and increasing the country's bargaining power in food trade and overseas agricultural investment. This is evidenced by its subdued response to the debates in the recent UN Food Systems Summit (Montenegro de Wit et al., 2021; Zhang, 2021). However, China's global food strategy may profoundly transform the international food order in the long term. First, China will become a major pole in the global food system in terms of food trade and agricultural technological innovation, which will erode the dominance of northern countries in these areas. Second, China will not undermine but actively support corporate rules in the global food system, as it relies on them to secure overseas food resources. It also has the ambition to build its own global agribusinesses, and this may intensify corporate competition, leading to the further penetration of corporate capital into food commodity frontiers. Third, as a food importer, China is interested in increasing the overall global food supply to create a food surplus situation. This will have both positive and negative effects on the food system. On the one hand, China may assist southern countries in reducing their food-import dependence through agricultural cooperation. On the other hand, this would exhaust food resources at a faster pace and exacerbate the vulnerability of the global food system.

China's global food strategy is fraught with limits and contradictions. To increase global food supply and maintain a high level of domestic production, the Chinese state seeks to build alliance with corporate capital, including state, private, and foreign capital. However, the long-term goal of food security runs in direct contradiction with the latter's short-term orientation for profit, contributing to speculations and crises in the food market. The influx of food imports and the expansion of domestic and foreign corporate capital will also disrupt the household mode of agricultural production in China, leading to exploitation and dispossession in the countryside and underemployment and precarity in the city, which in turn undermine food security at subnational and household levels. To maintain a high level of domestic production also means that China will continue to face great pressure from environmental degradation and resource constraints, which can easily disrupt the delicate balance between domestic food production and sourcing food beyond borders.

The following sections will unpack China's global food strategy and examine the various dimensions of the pursuit of an optimal national–global food duality. Section 2 examines the historical and contemporary contexts for the emergence of China's global food strategy. Section 3 analyzes China's food imports and agricultural trade. Section 4 focuses on China's overseas agricultural investment. Section 5 examines China's efforts to build global agribusiness corporations and the domestic origin of the state–capital alliance. Section 6 examines the impacts of the global food strategy on the agri-food system in China and the countermovements at the grassroots level, and Section 7 concludes this Element.

2 China's Global Food Strategy

2.1 Food Self-Sufficiency and Insufficiency (1949–1990)

Securing sufficient food for the population has been a top concern for the Chinese Communist Party (CCP). During the socialist period (1949–1976), the CCP was grappling with the problem of food shortages; a huge famine in 1959–1961, which resulted in millions of deaths, revealed how serious the problem was. As Chris Bramall noted, "the history of Chinese development during this period is, in many respects, a history of the search for solutions to this overriding problem (of food insecurity)" (2009: 213). Postwar geopolitics also played a role in shaping China's food policy as the United States and its allies imposed a total embargo on China. The breakup with the Soviet Union in 1959 had only made China's geopolitical environment worse. The international isolation forced the country to rely on domestic production for food. To increase domestic production, the CCP mobilized millions of peasants each year to construct irrigation facilities, expanding the irrigated area from 16 to 48 million hectares between 1949 and 1978 (Zhan, 2019a: 53). The party-state also made efforts to introduce agricultural technologies such as new farming methods, hybrid seeds, and chemical fertilizers to increase production (Schmalzer, 2016). As a result, the production of staple grain, the major food source, grew from 164 to 305 million tonnes between 1952 and 1978. However, the growth was largely neutralized by the doubling of the population. The annual consumption of cereals, beans, and tuber roots, which are classified as staple foods in Chinese official statistics, was 318 kilograms per capita in 1978, only slightly higher than 288 kilograms in 1952, but barely sufficient for the population of nearly 1 billion (Ministry of Agriculture [MOA], 2009: 14; National Bureau of Statistics [NBS], 2009: 37).[5]

In 1978, China launched rural reform, replacing collective farming with the Household Responsibility System (HRS) and introducing the market to the rural economy. Before, Chinese agriculture was based on a collective system, which consisted of three levels of collective units: the People's Communes, brigades, and production teams. The production team, each comprising twenty to thirty households, was the basic unit of production and distribution in the 1960s–1970s. The land was collectively owned and farmed, and individual peasant households could not cultivate land on their own. The collective system enabled rural communities to work together on public projects including irrigation; it also meant that under the system, rural surplus was transferred to urban industry through the sale of grain and other agricultural products to the state at fixed procurement prices (Bramall, 2009; Zhan, 2019a: 38–41). This reduced the incentive for peasants, particularly when procurement prices were low. Following rural reform, farmland was contracted to peasant households, which then held the use right of land, while the ownership still belonged to the village collective (the former brigade). Under the HRS, peasant households have the autonomy to farm the land on their own and engage in nonfarm activities.

Rural reform was followed by a surge in grain production, which increased by a third to 407 million tonnes in 1984, turning China into a net food exporter for the first time since the famine. The increase also lifted the annual consumption of grain to 392 kilograms per capita (Zhan, 2021). From then on, the figure has rarely fallen below 350 kilograms, which is sufficient to prevent another

---

[5] The per capita consumption of 318 kilograms of grain a year was sufficient to keep the Chinese population from starvation. But the structure of food consumption was dominated by grain, and the access to other food stuffs was quite limited, with only 11 kilograms of meat per person a year, 25 kilograms of sugar, 1 kilogram of milk, and 5 kilograms of aquatic products in 1978 (Ministry of Argiculture [MOA], 2009: 14).

nationwide food shortage or famine. Although the shift from collective farming to household production appeared to be a major factor behind the surge, researchers find that it was a result of multiple factors, including the use of chemical fertilizers, infrastructure improvement (irrigation in particular) in the socialist period, and the increase of grain procurement prices (Bramall, 2004; Schmalzer, 2016).

The increase in grain production boosted the legitimacy of the reformers within the CCP, but paradoxically it also tied their job performance to the sufficient supply of grain. Although agriculture accounted for a declining share in the economy in the 1980s–1990s, producing enough grain for the nation remained a key policy goal. Besides grain, other food products also experienced substantial growth in the 1980s. Between 1984 and 1990, the production of meat grew from 15.4 to 28.6 million tonnes, cow milk from 2.2 to 4.2 million tonnes, aquatic products from 6.2 to 12.4 million tonnes, sugar from 47.8 to 72.1 million tonnes, and fruits from 9.8 to 18.4 million tonnes (National Bureau of Statistics [NBS], 2009: 37–38). That is, within only six years, the supply of these foods had almost doubled. The rapid growth in these food products suggests that the dietary transition had begun in China as early as the 1980s as the population consumed more resource-intensive foods. The transition, however, was uneven across social classes and between rural and urban areas. For example, while the meat consumption of the rural population had increased, it lagged significantly behind that of urban consumers. In 1990, the consumption of meat per capita among urban residents was 25.2 kilograms, but an average rural resident consumed only half of this amount, 12.6 kilograms (National Bureau of Statistics [NBS], 1991: 289–303).

2.2 "Who Will Feed China" and the WTO Accession

The dietary transition captured Lester Brown's attention. He remarked, "Never in history have so many people moved up the food chain so fast" (Brown, 1995, 44). He was closely following China's food trade. An import of 6 million tonnes of grain to China in 1994, a negligible amount by China's food imports today, prompted him to write the sensational report *Who Will Feed China?* (Brown, 1995). Ironically, China was a food self-sufficient country and a food exporter at the time. In 1994, China exported 3 million tonnes more grain than it imported, and the value of total food exports also ran consistently higher than that of food imports throughout the 1990s (National Bureau of Statistics [NBS], 1999). Nevertheless, not only did the report bring global attention to China's food supply, but it also struck the nerve of the Chinese reformers who were highly concerned about grain production. In 1996, Chinese policy makers voluntarily pledged a 95 percent grain self-sufficiency ratio, that is, China would produce 95 percent of the staples (including cereals, beans, and tuber roots) that it consumes. The central government subsequently ramped up the efforts to boost grain production. One of the key measures was to increase grain procurement prices by 82 percent. As a result, grain production jumped to a new height, reaching 505 million tonnes in 1996 (National Bureau of Statistics [NBS], 2009: 37). Despite underestimating China's domestic production, Brown was prescient about its food problems. In addition to the dietary transition, he identified multiple factors that would undermine the capacity of China to feed itself, including environmental degradation, cropland loss, and water scarcity, which have been emphasized in subsequent studies on China's food security.

Brown limited his analysis to food supply and demand when predicting the devastating impact of massive grain imports to China on the global food system. He was silent, however, on how China could import such large quantities of grain. To address this question, one must examine the international political economy of food. In the same year when Brown published his report, the negotiations of the General Agreement on Tariffs and Trade (GATT) Uruguay Round (1986–1994) reached an agreement on agriculture. The agreement, called the "World Trade Organization (WTO) Agreement on Agriculture" after 1994, set the most important rules on international food trade. The agreement was to further liberalize agricultural trade and establish a free market for agricultural goods. Member nations were obliged to reduce tariffs on imports and cut export subsidies and other agricultural supports. It is argued that the agreement served the interests of corporate capital and developed countries while putting small farmers and developing countries at a disadvantage (McMichael, 2009; Patel, 2012). For example, the reduction of tariffs and the removal of trade and investment barriers opened the market in developing countries for global agribusiness corporations. The agreement also allows developed countries to maintain substantial subsidies and other domestic agricultural supports. As a result, the United States and European Union (EU) can sell agricultural commodities below the cost of production, which depresses global prices and hurts the agricultural exports of developing countries (Gonzalez, 2002; Clapp, 2006). The group who bears the brunt of the agreement may be small farmers in developing countries, many of whom are at risk of bankruptcy due to the low-priced imports and the high costs of agricultural inputs whose markets are controlled by agribusiness corporations (Shiva, 2001; Patel, 2012).

China was not a member nation of the WTO in the 1990s, but it was actively seeking to join it. The country applied for entry to the trade organization as early as 1986 (GATT at the time), and it was finally accepted as a WTO member in October 2001. To facilitate its acceptance to the WTO, China made more

Table 1 China's WTO commitments on food products subject to tariff rate quotas[6]

	Quota (million metric tonnes)			Out-of-quota tariff (%)		
	2002	**2004 and after**	**In-quota tariff (%)**	**2002**	**2003**	**2004 and after**
Rice	3.76	5.32	1	74	71	65
Wheat	8.45	9.46	1	71	68	65
Maize	5.70	7.20	1	71	68	65
Edible oils	5.69	6.81	9	75	71.7	68.3
Sugar	1.68	1.95	20	90	72	50

concessions than the trade organization would normally require for a regular developing country (Bhala, 1999; Liang, 2002). For example, the upper limit for domestic support for agriculture was 10 percent of the total annual value of agricultural production for developing countries and 5 percent for developed countries, but it was set at 8.5 percent for China. China also agreed to slash tariffs on agricultural imports within a much shorter timeline than required for a developing country (Table 1). The tariff on soybeans is a case in point. The country agreed to a 3 percent tariff, together with the removal of all import quotas on the commodity. The sharp lowering of tariffs on soybeans from 114 percent to 3 percent in 2000 led to soaring imports of the crop. The volume of soybean imports jumped from 4.3 million tonnes in 1999 to 10.4 million in 2000, and further to 20.7 million in 2003, up nearly four times in just four years. In 2001, China was a typical developing country in terms of agriculture, with 244 million farming households and farmland per capita of only 0.13 hectares in rural areas. Due to considerable concessions made on agriculture, observers were pessimistic about the prospect for Chinese agriculture at the time. Some predicted that its domestic grain production would decline by 20 percent due to massive imports after the WTO accession (Han, 2005).

The pledge on grain self-sufficiency and the accession to the WTO thus constitute a fundamental contradiction in China's food policy. To fulfil the self-sufficiency pledge, China must promote grain farming and produce enough domestic grain. Under the regulations of the WTO, however, China must open its market for the import of food commodities including grain, which will

---

[6] Table 1 is based on the data in Huang and Rozelle (2002). The quota regime on edible oils was phased out in 2006.

suppress domestic grain production. This contradiction has contributed to the formation of China's unique global food strategy in the 2000s. It should be noted that Brown's report was only partially responsible for the policy to promote domestic production. Grain farming provides a crucial source of livelihood for hundreds of millions of rural residents in China, thus any sharp decline in grain production would cause a livelihood crisis and stir social unrest (Christiansen, 2009; Zhan, 2021).

2.3 The Formation of China's Global Food Strategy

The year of 2004 marked a critical point in China's move toward a global food strategy. Between 1999 and 2003, annual domestic grain production experienced a five-year decline, down to 431 million tonnes. The decline started prior to the WTO accession and was mainly caused by domestic factors such as low market prices, heavy rural taxation, and low consumer demand after the 1997 financial crisis. The decline was also associated with a general rural crisis, which triggered widespread rural unrest and resistance (Wen, 2001; Bernstein and Lü, 2003; O'Brien and Li, 2006). Worse, as required by the WTO, China had to substantially cut tariffs in 2004 for a range of agricultural products, including cereals (Table 1), which could further undermine agricultural production. Alarmed by the rural crisis and pressed under the WTO obligations, the Chinese state was forced to promote domestic production to improve the rural situation and offset the impacts of the WTO accession. While China resembled other developing countries in terms of having a smallholder agriculture, it had an advantage that most developing countries did not. Since 1978, the country had experienced rapid industrial and urban growth for more than two decades and expanded fiscal capacity to the extent that it was able to subsidize agriculture, which was usually practiced in developed countries. In early 2004, the central government announced the abolition of all agricultural taxes and fees, and by 2006, farmers nationwide were free of agricultural taxes. Furthermore, the government started to provide direct subsidies for small farmers, aiming to alleviate the rural crisis and enhance their incentive for grain production. Besides tax abolition and subsidies, the Chinese state has implemented many other prorural policies, to be further discussed later.

The WTO accession compels China to open the market for agricultural imports and foreign investments, but the country has some room to protect domestic production. The cereals including rice, wheat, and corn are protected by tariff rate quotas (TRQs). The annual quotas for the import of rice, wheat, and corn are 5.3 million tonnes, 9.6 million tonnes, and 7.2 million tonnes after 2004, respectively. The in-quota imports will be charged at a tariff of only

1 percent, whereas the out-of-quota imports are subjected to 65 percent (Table 1). In addition, China can provide price support for agriculture as long as the amount of support does not exceed 8.5 percent of annual agricultural output. The supportive measures in the Green Box, which are considered to cause minimal or no distortion to trade, are exempt from the limit (World Trade Organization [WTO], 2022). The examples of these measures include direct payments to producers, income insurance and income safety-net programs, and payments under environmental programs.

Nevertheless, the WTO trade regime removed many barriers to the Chinese market, leading to growing volumes and number of varieties of foods exported to the country. The rising demand for resource-intensive foods, such as meat, dairy, sugar, and fruits, has also fuelled the trend. In the 2000s, it had become increasingly clear that China could not keep the pledge of the 95 percent grain self-sufficiency ratio for long. For example, soybeans, mainly used for animal feed and oils, have flooded into the Chinese market under a 3 percent tariff rate. Soybeans were included in the basket of grain under the self-sufficiency grain policy, and its soaring imports quickly drove down China's self-sufficiency ratio. In 2008, the soybean imports reached 37.4 million tonnes, decreasing the grain self-sufficiency ratio to below 95 percent for the first time since the mid-1990s. In 2017, before the US–China trade war, China imported a record 95.5 million tonnes of soybeans and 25.6 million tonnes of cereals, with a self-sufficiency ratio of only 84.7 percent (Figure 1). In 2008, there were rumors that China would discard the grain self-sufficiency policy, as the country was about to release a grain security guideline document for the period of 2008–2020. However, the adjustment was delayed until 2013. Nevertheless, the 2008 guideline document, titled "Outline of the Medium- and Long-Term Plan for National Food Security (2008–2020)" (The State Council, 2008), acknow-ledged a range of challenges on food security, including rising demand, diet upgrading, farmland loss, water scarcity, environmental constraints, and a volatile global market. The document mainly focuses on domestic measures for solutions, such as promoting domestic production, increasing the level of grain stocking, and improving the functions of food markets. Food imports and international agricultural cooperation are also identified as a solution, but the document stresses that this should be supplementary.

In a meeting on rural affairs in December 2013, the Chinese central govern-ment finally revised the dysfunctional grain self-sufficiency policy. The new policy signalled the active implementation of China's new global food strategy that aims to optimize the national–global food duality. The new policy has made three major changes. First, it adjusted the self-sufficiency grain basket by removing soybeans and root tubers and only including cereals including rice,

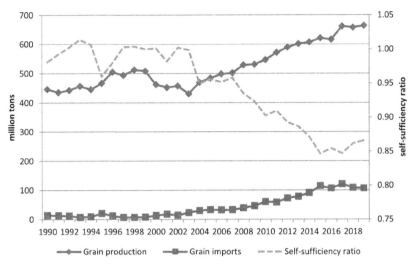

Figure 1 China's grain production, grain imports, and self-sufficiency ratio: 1990–2019[7]

wheat, and corn. Second, the new policy emphasizes the active utilization of the global market and overseas agricultural resources, and approves "moderate imports" (适度进口) to meet the growing domestic demand. The new policy also encourages domestic agribusiness enterprises to "go out" and compete globally. Third, the new policy downplays, to some extent, the quantity of domestic grain production and instead stresses the importance of agricultural production capacity. Under this new guideline, policies are implemented to preserve agricultural resources and allow some areas of farmland to lie fallow for environmental protection.

In the following years, the new global food strategy has been refined and elaborated. For instance, there has been a growing emphasis on integrating the global food strategy with the BRI and promoting agricultural cooperation with the countries that joined the BRI. The 2018 "No.1 Central Document" (*Xinhua*, 2018a) proposed that Chinese global grain marketing firms and agribusiness corporations should be promoted, and the document also stressed the need to actively participate in global food security governance and the rulemaking process in international agricultural trade. The policies since 2016 reiterated the sustainable use of farmland and the critical role of agricultural technology, literally summarized as "maintaining grain production capacity in farmland and technology" (藏粮于地, 藏粮于技). It should be noted that the strategy of

---

[7] The data is derived from the *China Statistical Yearbook* (various years). The grain in the figure include cereals, soybeans, and root tubers.

optimizing the national–global food duality does not move unidirectionally toward the increasing use of external agricultural resources but is adjusted to balance domestic production and overseas supply. For example, as the US–China trade war created uncertainties for agricultural imports, the Chinese state once again set the quantitative target of annual domestic grain production in 2019, which should be maintained above 650 million tonnes (Qiao, 2019). The efforts to achieve the goal only intensified in 2020 as the COVID-19 pandemic disrupted the global food trading system, even though the country imported more grain in 2020 than previous years. With the increasing volatility of the global market, the goal was written into the 2022 "No.1 Central Document" on agriculture and rural affairs.[8]

2.4 Key Components of China's Global Food Strategy

China's global food strategy does not seek to maximize food imports. This is an observation different from what most studies on the country's food strategy would suggest. Neither will (or can) it reinstitute the food self-sufficiency policy. Rather, the country aims to achieve an optimal national–global food duality by pursuing three interlinked goals: stability, control, and leverage. Stability means that China strives to achieve stable supplies of food both domestically and internationally and safeguard against the disruptions of these supplies. Control refers to the control of tangible and intangible food resources including farmland, processing and warehousing facilities, agricultural technology, trade routes, and an advantageous position in the global food market. Leverage refers to maintaining high levels of domestic production and stocking to leverage on the use of overseas resources. With a high level of domestic supply, China can adjust import categories and amounts, and gain an advantageous position in bargaining for agri-food deals or use food imports and assistance as a means for geopolitical influence. Revolving around these three goals, China's global food strategy comprises six key components.

- *Diversifying the sources of food imports.* The diversification of food imports is a common strategy of food-importing countries to ensure supply stability. This is because with multiple import sources, a country could mitigate the impacts once the imports from one or more sources were disrupted. However, there are only a small number of large food exporters but a much greater number of food-importing countries. Thus, the food-importing countries are usually at a disadvantage when facing a tight global market. For instance, the source countries of soybean exports are concentrated in the Americas, with

---

[8] The document (in Chinese) can be accessed at www.gov.cn/zhengce/2022-02/22/content_/ 5675035.htm.

the United States and Brazil accounting for more than 80 percent of soybean exports in recent years (Gale et al., 2019). Soybeans are a major food commodity that China imports. The country has been trying to create new sources of soybean imports, but with very limited success. For instance, there was a proposal to boost soybean imports from Russia (*Beijing News*, 2019), but it is estimated that Russia could only export 10 million tonnes at most in the future, accounting for about 10 percent of China's imports. Rice is another example. The leading rice exporters are India, Thailand, and Vietnam. China mainly depends on domestic production for rice, but it also seeks to turn Myanmar, Cambodia, and Laos into new sources of imports. The strategy of diversifying imports will be detailed in Section 3.

- *Enhancing the infrastructure of food supply to China, including trade networks and infrastructural facilities.* As a food importer, China is concerned about the disruption of supply chains and logistics. To reduce such risks, the country has signed 120 bilateral and multilateral agreements on food and agriculture with more than sixty countries and international organizations (The State Council, 2019). One of the purposes for launching the BRI in 2013 was to enhance the infrastructure of international trade. China has invested in railways, ports, airports, waterways, and food processing and warehousing facilities in BRI countries, which could reduce the risk of blockade in international logistic routes. For example, the Strait of Malacca and the Suez Canal are critical "chokepoints" of trade routes between Western and Asian markets, and a large share of China's international shipments including food imports and exports are transported through there (Bailey and Wellesley, 2017). The infrastructure projects under the BRI would build alternative trade routes to connect China with countries in Europe, Central Asia, and South and Southeast Asia (Tortajada and Zhang, 2021).

- *Acquiring and developing modern agricultural technologies.* Agricultural technology assumes a prominent place in China's food strategy. Given limited land and water resources, China has been keen to increase the output per unit of land and water, and it is particularly interested in developing high-yield seeds and water-saving technologies. In recent years, China has outspent the United States on agricultural research and development (R&D) by some measures (Chai et al., 2019), and this investment frenzy manifests in the slogan of "promoting grain production through technology" (藏粮于技). Following the WTO accession, China has taken note of how the control of agricultural technology gives agribusiness conglomerates a powerful position in the global food system. In addition to developing its own agricultural technologies, the country has been actively seeking to acquire international agribusiness companies to access and control technological know-how.

The acquisition of Syngenta by ChemChina in 2016 was a case in point. Syngenta was a global agrichemical giant specializing in genetically modified (GM) seeds and agriculture protection technologies such as pesticide and herbicide (Bratspies, 2017). By acquiring Syngenta with a record US$43 billion, ChemChina hoped to gain access to the company's technologies and take advantage of its global market reach.

- *Encouraging overseas agricultural investment.* China's overseas agricultural investment has grown rapidly after the country launched the "going out" strategy in 1999. Although agriculture accounts for less than 2 percent of China's total overseas investment, it appears a fast-growing area of investment in the future (Zhan et al., 2018). China is keen to utilize overseas agricultural resources to meet domestic food demand, but the direct control of land and water resources seems not to be a priority. A careful analysis of Chinese overseas agricultural investments reveals that these investments are mainly aimed at increasing production and making profits (see Section 4). The Chinese state particularly holds a productivist doctrine, arguing that the overall increase in production benefits both China and the host country and thus it is a "win-win" solution. Specifically, the increase in production will meet the host country's domestic demand if it is a food-deficient country or boost food exports if it is a food exporter. In both cases, China will gain as a major food importer by increasing food supply and reducing competition for imports in the global market.
- *Participating in and influencing global food governance.* China has been actively participating in global food security governance. First, it joined international and regional organizations on food governance and participated in the agenda setting and rulemaking processes. For instance, China raised food security governance as an important issue for the G-20's agenda (Duggan and Naarajärvi, 2015). And the country also endorsed the initiative to build an ASEAN (Association of Southeast Asian Nations) Plus Three Emergency Rice Reserve after the 2007/2008 food crisis. In 2019, Qu Dongyu, a Deputy Minister for Agriculture and Rural Affairs for China, was elected Director-General of the Food and Agriculture Organization of the UN (FAO). Second, it provides food aid and agricultural development assistance programs to developing countries to improve bilateral relations on agricultural cooperation (Morton, 2012). Last, it strives to create its own global agribusiness giants to influence and benefit from the corporate governance of the global food system. It should be noted that, although China has been actively promoting bilateral and multilateral food cooperation, the country appears less interested in challenging the existing rules or regulations in the global food system. This is evidenced by its low-profile presence in the recent UN Food Systems Summit (Zhang, 2021).

- *Maintaining a high level of domestic food production.* This is so that it could withhold, at least for a short period, the disruption of food imports, and this enhances China's position and leverage in the global market. Maintaining domestic production ensures that China will not be in a powerless position even though it must depend on imports to meet food demand. As noted earlier, due to the trade war and the impact of the pandemic, China again set the quantitative target for domestic production. The target of annual production above 650 million tonnes is likely to meet more than 80 percent of China's consumption of grain, including both stable and feed grain. In addition, it attempts to strengthen the grain stocking system, and to store the amounts of grain sufficient for at least half a year's domestic consumption. Other measures to support agriculture and grain production include protecting farmland, enhancing farmers' incentives to produce grain, providing direct subsidies for agricultural production, offering price protection for key crops, and supporting agricultural exports.

3 Will China Starve the World? China in Agri-Food Trade

Food trade occupies a central place in China's global food strategy. The scholarship on China's food trade is copious, and most focuses on soaring food imports to the country. An underlying assumption in many studies is that China's imports would adversely affect global food security, particularly food security in low-income countries, as the country competes for food in the global market. China's growing propensity for rich-diet foods is also a focus of research. The country is the largest importer of soybeans and a key player in the global soybean–livestock complex (Weis, 2013), and it also imports large volumes of meat, edible oils, dairy products, seafood, and tropical fruits. While food imports to China have clearly altered international food trade relations, it is less obvious how China's imports have affected (or will affect) global food security. Will China's food imports starve the world, as Brown's question "who will feed China" suggests? An apparent puzzle on China's food trade is that China was able to use "import refusals" in the recent trade war with the United States and the disputes with other large food exporters such as Canada and Australia. This defies the notion of China's extreme food-import dependence, which assumes that China has no choice but import as much as it can.

Another deficiency in the literature is that it often takes for granted the functioning of a *free* global food market and suggests that food will be exported to countries that offer higher prices. Although free market rules have dominated international food trade in the past decades, the assumption does not always hold true. During the 2007/2008 food crisis and the early phase of the COVID-19 pandemic, a number of food exporters imposed export embargos to prioritise domestic food needs. This suggests that international food imports and exports in a situation of food shortages or crises will not be regulated by a free global food market but by complex geopolitics and the political economy of nations. The possibility of trade disruption, which looks increasingly likely in a period of rising trade tensions, economic protectionism, disease outbreaks, and frequent natural disasters due to climate change, has forced many countries including China to evaluate their strategies on food trade and domestic production. For example, there has been a reemphasis on domestic production and self-sufficiency in food-importing countries after the 2007/2008 food crisis (Clapp, 2017).

This section situates China in a changing global food system and examines the emerging patterns of the country's food trade. It first discusses the new trends in the global food system and how these both created opportunities for and imposed constraints on China's food trade. The analysis shows that the liberalization of food trade, which McMichael (2009) regards as the transition to a corporate food regime, and the rise of new agricultural countries (NACs) have allowed China to diversify the sources of food imports. Additionally, the emergence of new exporters in the Global South and the expanding South–South agri-food trade have contributed to China's growing food imports from the global market, and vice versa. China's food trade has also been significantly shaped by domestic food conditions. The self-sufficiency of cereals has greatly reduced the need to import these commodities, in contrast to the soaring imports of soybeans. The massive soybean imports should first and foremost be attributed to China's high demand for meat and edible oils, but it has also been a result of the policy decision that regards soybeans as less strategically important than cereals in the country's food security governance. The robust production of meat, milk, fruits, and vegetables within China has to some extent lessened the need to import these food products, and the country has also expanded agri-food exports, particularly aquatic products, fruits, and vegetables, which offsets the deficits in international food trade.

3.1 Liberalization of Food Trade and Rise of NACs

The neoliberal turn in the world economy since the 1970s profoundly transformed the global food system. The role of transnational agribusiness and free market rules have risen to dominance, subjecting the states and farmers to the world market and depriving them of food sovereignty (Pechlaner and Otero, 2008; Patel, 2012). McMichael (2009) argues that the global food system has transitioned into a corporate food regime, under which the interest of corporate capital, with the support of the state, overrides those of producers and consumers. According to him, this corporate food regime was born out of structural adjustments in the 1980s. Since the 1990s, the WTO has reinforced the regime by removing barriers to trade and foreign investment under the Agreement on Agriculture, and this is supplemented by bilateral and multilateral free trade agreements (McMichael, 2009). The neoliberal ideology of market fundamentalism, propagated by the World Bank and WTO and large food exporters such as the United States has also played a role in the liberalization of food trade. The ideology spreads the notion that food trade, rather than domestic production or self-sufficiency, is the best way to achieve a country's food security.

When China joined the WTO in 2001, the food system based on corporate power and free market rules was already in place to regulate the country's involvement in international food trade. The low tariffs under the WTO have facilitated the import of food products to China, particularly crops and products whose offshore prices are lower than China's domestic prices. Furthermore, transnational agribusiness corporations, which control market networks for global sourcing, are ready to ship large volumes of food commodities to China. The soybean trade is a case in point. In the 2000s, the soybeans imported from the Americas to China were sourced and sold by large transnational grain merchants, known as the ABCD group, that is, ADM Co., Bunge Ltd. and Cargill Inc. from the United States, and the Netherlands-based Louis Dreyfus Company. This was described as "South America produces soybeans, China buys soybeans, and the ABCD sells soybeans" (Zhang, 2018: 236).

The rise of NACs since the late 1970s has also shaped China's international food trade. The NACs in Latin America, Asia, and Africa, such as Brazil, Chile, Argentina, South Africa, Thailand, India, Vietnam, and Indonesia, have carved out a significant share in the agri-food export market (Friedmann, 1992; Fold and Pritchard, 2005). The NACs have eroded the dominance of the United States and the EU in the export market, and this intensifies the competition among exporters, to the advantage of food-importing countries including China. For example, the United States accounted for more than 50 percent of the world wheat market in the early 1970s and enjoyed a near monopoly over soybean exports (Friedmann, 1982; Zhang, 2018: 45); by 2018, however, its shares in global wheat and soybean exports had decreased to 15 and 37 percent, respectively (Observatory of Economic Complexity [OEC], 2021). During the trade war, China was able to reduce soybean imports from the United States by 50 percent in 2018 and made up the shortage with more imports from Brazil and Argentina (Liu et al., 2020). The rise of NACs has also provided China with multiple import sources of food products such as meat, dairy, fruits, and aquatic products so that China will not be too dependent on a particular country.

Table 2 reports the key food commodities exported to China in 2019, their source countries, and their market share. The NACs in Latin America, including Brazil, Argentina, Ecuador, and Uruguay, have significantly contributed to China's imports of soybeans, meat, and seafood. This reduced the shares of the United States, Australia, and Canada in the export market to China. The NACs in Asia, such as India, Thailand, Vietnam, the Philippines, and Indonesia, have taken up a significant market share in seafood, fish, and tropical fruits. China also started to import fish and cerals from Eastern Europe and Central Asia, such as Russia, Ukraine, and Kazakhstan. The EU changed from a food importer to a net food exporter in food trade with China in the past decade, as the EU member states increased the exports of meat, fish, and dairy products to the country (Pawlak et al., 2016). The data also reveal that China imported a much smaller value of cereals than that of soybeans, and the sources of cereal imports were also diversified between American, European, and Asian countries. Australia and New Zealand exported significant amounts of dairy products and meat to China.

3.2 South–South Food Trade and China's Import Diversification

Between 1970 and 2000, the percentages of agri-food exports from Africa, Latin America and the Caribbean, and the least developed countries have declined or stagnated, whereas the share of northern countries has increased (Aksoy, 2004; McMichael, 2005: 279; Pritchard, 2009: 301). Since the new millennium, however, the share of the Global South in world agri-food exports has significantly increased, largely due to the rise of emerging economies.

According to the FAO (2018), the world agri-food trade increased more than threefold in value from 2000 to 2016, much faster than the growth of world GDP. The expansion in both supply and demand from emerging economies was a major factor behind the growth. China increased its share in world food imports from 2.3 to 8.2 percent, while other emerging economies such as India, Indonesia, and Russia increased their aggregate share from 3.4 to 5.2 percent. The emerging economies also enlarged their proportions in the global export market. The aggregate share of Brazil, China, India, and Indonesia in food exports increased from 8.5 to 14.5 percent during this period. In contrast, developed economies including the United States, EU, Japan, and Australia have seen their shares in imports and exports declining. The increasing

Table 2 Key food commodities exported to China in 2019: Source countries and market shares[9]

Key food imports	Value (billion US$)	Top exporters and their market shares in exports to China (%)						
Soybeans	32.1	Brazil 63.7	United States 24.5	Argentina 9.4	Uruguay 1.6	Russia 0.6	Canada 0.1	
Frozen bovine meat	8.9	Brazil 30.0	Argentina 23.1	Australia 17.9	Uruguay 12.5	New Zealand 11.6	Canada 0.8	United States 0.8
Crustaceans	6.3	Ecuador 32.9	India 15	Canada 9.6	Australia 8.3	New Zealand 3.4	Thailand 3.0	
Pig meat	5.9	Spain 21.0	Germany 14.7	United States 14.5	Brazil 10.4	Denmark 10.1	Netherlands 8.7	Canada 6.2
Concentrated milk	4.1	New Zealand 56.6	Hong Kong[10] 19.2	Australia 6.9	Netherlands 2.6	France 1.9	United Kingdom 1.8	Germany 1.7
Frozen fish	4.8	Russia 27.6	United States 12.5	Norway 8.2	India 6.3	Greenland 3.8	South Korea 3.7	Indonesia 3.6
Tropical fruits	1.1	Thailand 36.7	Vietnam 26.3	Philippines 12.2	Hong Kong 6.9	Taiwan 6.7	Indonesia 2.0	
Wheat	1.2	Canada 61.4	France 10.8	Kazakhstan 8.4	Australia 7.9	United States 6.3	Lithuania 4.2	Russia 0.9
Rice	1.4	Myanmar 28.7	Thailand 21.4	Pakistan 18.6	Vietnam 16.8	Cambodia 12.0	Taiwan 1.3	Laos 1.0
Corn	1.0	Ukraine 76.9	Myanmar 10.0	United States 5.6	Laos 2.6	Bulgaria 2.0	Brazil 1.1	Russia 1.0
Starches	1.0	Thailand 64.4	Vietnam 28.6	Netherlands 1.9	Cambodia 1.8	Germany 0.8	Belgium 0.5	Laos 0.5

[9] The data is derived from the Observatory of Economic Complexity (OEC) (2021). The OEC is an online data visualization and distribution platform focused on the geography and dynamics of economic activities. The data of the OEC primarily comes from the UN Comtrade database.

[10] Hong Kong does not produce concentrated milk but reexports its imports to mainland China. Hong Kong's main source countries in concentrated milk are as follows: Netherlands (22.2%), China (16.9%), Ireland (16.3%), New Zealand (11.6%), Germany (10.9%), Australia (7.7%), and Switzerland (3.2%).

importance of emerging economies significantly altered food trade patterns of the Global South. Agri-food exports from middle- and low-income countries increased from 9.4 to 20.1 percent of the global agricultural trade value between 2000 and 2015,[11] and exports to these countries followed a similar trend. Meanwhile, the South–South trade, that is, food trade among middle- and low-income countries, increased in weightage. In 2000, these countries sourced 41.9 percent of their food management imports from other southern countries, and this figure increased to 54.4 percent in 2015. In terms of exports, more than half went to other southern countries in 2015, an increase from less than 40 percent in 2000 (Food and Agriculture Organization of the UN [FAO], 2018: 5–7).

China has been a major factor behind the growing importance of the Global South in the world food economy. Although the country must depend on large Western food exporters such as the United States, Canada, and Australia for much of its food imports, it has been actively seeking new sources of imports in the Global South. For example, China signed a free trade agreement with ASEAN in 2002, and this led to rapid growth in agri-food trade between China and Southeast Asian countries (Zhan et al., 2018). In 2019, Southeast Asia was the second largest exporter to China, behind Brazil but ahead of the EU, the United States, and Australia. Figure 2 shows that agri-food exports to China grew rapidly in value between 2000 and 2020, up from US$9.2 billion to US$161 billion. The exports from five major Western food exporters, including the United States, Canada, the EU, Australia, and New Zealand, also grew from US$5.6 billion to US$52 billion. However, the share of the five exporters significantly declined from 61 percent to 32 percent. This means that China sourced an increasing share of agri-food imports from other countries.

China has been actively seeking new sources of food imports. In Southeast Asia, for example, the country increased rice imports from Myanmar, Cambodia, and Laos, which became rice exporters in the 2000s due to both productivity growth and high demand from China. As a result, China is able to diversify rice imports beyond the traditional exporters. From 2011 to 2020, China looked to Russia and other countries in Central Asia and Eastern Europe for cereal imports, particularly wheat and corn (Zhang, 2018: 181–182). China's cereal imports from these countries lessened its dependence on the United States and Canada. Table 2 shows that Ukraine became the largest exporter of corn to China in 2019, accounting for 76.9 percent, whereas the United States ranked the third, making up only 5.6 percent (down from 18.8 percent in 2017 due to the trade war). Kazakhstan, Lithuania, and Russia were also major

---

[11] The denominator comprises both import and export values, thus the percentages seem low.

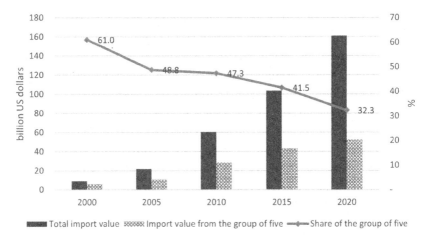

Figure 2 Agri-food imports to China from the world and from the group of five (United States, Canada, the EU, Australia, and New Zealand) in 2000–2020[12]

exporters of wheat to China in 2019. The Commonwealth of Independent States, that is, an organization that includes many countries from the former Soviet Union, has emerged as a major exporter of cereals since the 1990s (Krausmann and Langthaler, 2019). During the last decade, China's demand became a key factor behind their export expansion. Africa is not a major food exporter to China as the continent relies on imports for food, particularly cereals and meat. From 2011 to 2020, the exports from Africa to China mainly comprise nonstaple food products, including ground nuts (Senegal, Ethiopia, and Sudan), coffee (Ethiopia, Uganda, and Kenya), other oily seeds (Sudan, Niger, Ethiopia, and Tanzania, etc.), and citrus fruits (Egypt and South Africa). The values of these exports were modest, mostly less than US$1 billion for each category in 2019 (Observatory of Economic Complexity [OEC], 2021).

The expansion of South–South food trade has both been caused by and contributed to China's import diversification. China still relies on major Western exporters for soybeans, meat (beef in particular), and dairy products, but it has found new sources of supply in the NACs and other southern countries.[13] The growing demand in China for nonstaple food products, such as fruits, vegetables, nuts, and aquatic products, has provided a new export market for southern countries, which increased the latter's market share in food exports. The question remains whether China will also be a competitor for food and affect food imports for these countries, particularly

---

[12] Data source: UN Comtrade data, https://comtrade.un.org/.
[13] The US–China phase one deal in 2019 will increase China's agricultural imports from the United States, but China is likely to continue import diversification.

low-income countries. The next subsection will partly address this question by examining the relations between China's domestic production and international trade.

3.3 Domestic Conditions and Food Trade

Table 2 shows a great difference between soybeans and cereals in terms of import value. In 2019, China imported US$32.1 billion worth of soybeans, but only US$4.6 billion of three major cereals and starches. This is primarily due to the difference between soybeans and cereals in domestic supply. The production of rice, corn, and wheat in China was 210, 261, and 134 million tonnes in 2019, respectively, whereas the production of soybeans was only 18 million tonnes (National Bureau of Statistics [NBS], 2020). In addition, China maintains massive stockpiles of rice and wheat, which could meet the needs of domestic consumption for a year.[14] Computed based on domestic production and net imports, the self-sufficiency ratios of rice, corn, wheat, and soybeans in 2019 were 98.5, 98.2, 98.4, and 17.0 percent, respectively (Ministry of Agriculture and Rural Affairs [MOARA], 2020a; National Bureau of Statistics [NBS], 2020).

The difference in domestic supply between cereals and soybeans has much to do with China's grain policy. In the 1990s, during the negotiations over the WTO accession, China gave in to the demand of the United States for low tariff rates on soybeans, even though the crop was included in the self-sufficiency grain basket at the time. The soybean has been a fast-growing export crop since the end of World War II, with the United States being a leading exporter. Soybeans are mainly used for animal feed and the production of oil, constituting the oilseed–livestock complex for the prosperity diet (Friedmann, 1992; Weis, 2013). Although vital in producing animal protein, the crop is nevertheless considered less strategic than cereals in China's national food security,[15] evidenced by stagnant production, massive imports, and the removal of the crop from the self-sufficiency basket in 2013. Furthermore, soybeans are a land-intensive crop, with lower yields per unit of land. The average yield of soybeans is around 3 tonnes per hectare, whereas a yield of corn can reach 15 tonnes per hectare. Thus, China, a farmland-scarce country, has chosen to prioritize corn over soybeans due to the former's higher yield. Between 1994 and 2019, China's grain

---

[14] The corn stockpile was also massive in size before 2017, but it shrunk rapidly after that due to the destocking policy.

[15] An interesting precedent is that the European Economic Community exempted soybeans from import duties in the negotiations with the US in the 1960s, in exchange for the protection of the wheat sector (Friedmann, 1992: 377).

production (including cereals, beans, and root tubers) increased from 445 to 664 million tonnes, of which the production of wheat increased from 99 to 134 million tonnes, rice from 135 to 210 million tonnes, and corn from 99 to 261 million tonnes. In contrast, soybean production decreased from 16 million tonnes in 1994 to 12 million tonnes in 2015 before rising to 18 million tonnes in 2019 (Ministry of Agriculture [MOA], 2009: 17–22; National Bureau of Statistics [NBS], 2020). The data also reveal that corn accounted for 74 percent of the overall growth of grain production for the period of 1994–2019. Under a grain policy that prioritizes the aggregate production of grain crops, it is unsurprising that corn has outcompeted soybeans for land in main production areas in China, particularly in northeast regions (Heilongjiang, Jilin, Liaoning, and Inner Mongolia).

Besides cereals, China has managed to increase the production of a range of other foods in the past two decades by means of expanding irrigation, promoting intensive industrial livestock production, and applying agricultural technologies. Between 2001 and 2020, the outputs of sugar crops, vegetables, and fruits increased from 87 to 120 million tonnes (up 38 percent), 484 to 749 million tonnes (up 55 percent), and 67 to 287 million tonnes (up 328 percent), respectively. Meanwhile, the production of meat, mostly pork, increased from 61 to 77 million tonnes,[16] edible oils from 29 to 36 million tonnes, milk from 10 to 34 million tonnes, eggs from 22 to 35 million tonnes, and aquatic products from 38 to 65 million tonnes (National Bureau of Statistics [NBS], 2021a). The dramatic growth has led scholars to argue that China experienced a hidden agricultural revolution (Huang, 2016). The growth in domestic production of these products has to some extent reduced the scale of imports.

Table 3 shows that despite increasing imports, China maintains high self-sufficiency ratios for most key food products. The self-sufficiency ratios of sugar, nuts, vegetables, fruits, meat, eggs, milk, fish and seafood, and stimulants were all above 90 percent in 2018. The ratios of bovine meat and vegetable oils were 83 and 74 percent, respectively. It should be noted that the massive imports of soybeans, whose self-sufficiency ratio was below 15 percent in 2018, contributed to the production of pig meat, which reached 54 million tonnes. Thus, the actual self-sufficiency ratio of pig meat should be much lower than what appears in Table 3. Suppose that meat production in China would decrease by 30 million tonnes without soybean imports, an estimate based on the meat production of 61 million tonnes in 2001, when

---

[16] The production increase in pork and edible oil should be largely attributed to massive imports of soybeans, and that pork production decreased from 54 million tonnes in 2018 to 41 million tonnes in 2020 due to the outbreak of African swine fever.

Table 3 Domestic production and net imports of key food products in China in 2018[17]

Food products (million tonnes)					
	Sugar and sweeteners	Nuts and nut products	Vegetable oils	All vegetables	All fruits	All meats
Production	13.0	3.8	25.1	624.5	165.2	86.0
Net imports	1.4	0.1	9.0	-13.9	0.6	2.8
Self-sufficiency ratio	0.90	0.97	0.74	1.02	~1.00	0.97

Food products	Bovine meat	Poultry	Eggs	Milk	Fish and seafood	Stimulants
Production	6.4	19.4	31.3	35.2	61.1	2.7
Net imports	1.3	-0.9	-0.1	1.1	3.5	-0.3
Self-sufficiency ratio	0.83	~1.00	~1.00	0.97	0.95	1.11

17 Data is drawn from FAO Food Balance Sheets, www.fao.org/faostat/en/#data/FBS.

the volume of soybean imports was low (14 million tonnes), it can be estimated that the actual self-sufficiency ratio of meat in China was approximately 63 percent in 2018.[18]

High levels of domestic production in China have reduced the scale of imports in cereals, vegetables, poultry, and eggs, whereas inadequate production of soybeans, bovine meat, milk, and edible oils spurred the needs for imports. It should be noted that food imports also serve to diversify diets as some products are imported not to feed the population but to meet the demand for new tastes among affluent consumers. China has been a leading producer and exporter of fish and seafood but it also imports large volumes of aquatic products from other countries. The same holds true for fruits as the country, despite being the largest fruit producer, imports a range of exotic fruits to meet the domestic demand for new tastes. Avocado is a case in point. The fruit was relatively unknown in China until the 2010s. In 2011, China imported 31.8 tonnes of avocados, but the volume soared to 44,000 tonnes in 2018 before declining to 33,000 tonnes in 2019 (Fresh Plaza, 2020).

3.4 China as a Food Exporter

China is a major food exporter and was once regarded as an NAC (Fold and Pritchard, 2005: 4). The country exported US$74 billion worth of food in 2020, ranking fourth in the world, behind the EU, the United States, and Brazil. Although not as dramatic as food imports, China's food exports have also experienced considerable growth in the past two decades. Between 2000 and 2020, the value of China's food exports increased from US$15 billion to US$74 billion (Figure 3). In the past five years (2016–2020), however, the growth in food exports slowed down, increasing by only US$7 billion. This contrasted with the strong growth in the value of imports, up from US$103 billion to US$161 billion. The diverging trend of exports and imports increased China's food trade deficit to US$87 billion in 2020.

China is a major exporter of fish and seafood, fruits, and vegetables. Based on the analysis of UN Comtrade data, the top categories of China's food exports in 2020 include i. fish, crustaceans, molluscs, and other fish products (15 percent of total exports); ii. edible vegetables, and certain roots and tubers (13 percent); iii. preparations of meat, fish, crustaceans, and other animal products (12 percent); iv. edible fruit and nuts (10 percent); and v. preparations of vegetables,

---

[18] A total of 30 million tonnes of meat in domestic production were regarded as imports. The new ratio is computed by dividing domestic production (56 million tonnes) by total consumption (88.8 million tonnes).

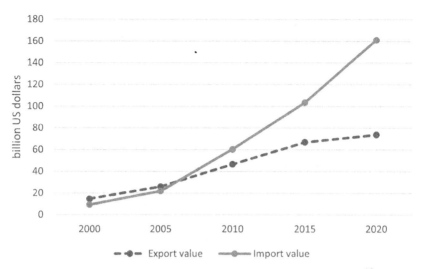

Figure 3 China's total food imports and exports: 2000–2020[19]

fruits, and nuts (10 percent). Taken together, these five categories account for 60 percent of total exports.

Food exports play a significant role in shaping China's food trade and domestic production. The large volume of exports to some extent offset China's food trade deficit and further integrated the country into the global food system. Food exports also offer a source of employment and income for the Chinese rural population, whose livelihood has been under great stress due to large imports of land-intensive products to the country.

3.5 Assessment of China's Food Imports

The literature has mainly focused on domestic demand and supply to explain soaring food imports to China over the past two decades. While resource constraints and dietary transition have indeed played a key role, the previous analysis in this section shows that food imports to China have also been conditioned by the restructuring of the global food system. The liberalization of food trade, characterized by the global reach of corporate capital and the dominance of free market rules, has created a global market for China to import food after its accession to the WTO in 2001. The rise of NACs in Latin America and Asia has provided China with alternative import sources for soybeans, meat, and horticultural products. China's food imports have also contributed to the restructuring of the global food system. China's efforts of import

---

[19] Data source: UN Comtrade data, https://comtrade.un.org/.

diversification, and the growing weightage of the country and other emerging markets in the world food economy, stimulated food exports from middle- and low-income countries in the Global South; this reversed the declining share of food exports for these countries in the 1980s and 1990s. How will China's food trade affect global food security? The previous analysis provides the basis for some preliminary assessments.

First, China has emerged as a new center in the global oilseed–livestock complex. By importing more than 60 percent of the soybeans in the global market, China is a driving force behind the expansion of the crop in the Americas, most importantly in Brazil, the United States, and Argentina. The encroachment on the forestry by the crop in the Amazon will have a long-term impact on the global environment, which in turn will affect crop production in the region and beyond (Fuchs et al., 2019). In addition, China has actively sought to create new sources of production in other countries for import diversification. If successful, we will likely witness the expansion of the crop in Russia, Ukraine, and African countries.

Second, it is unlikely that China would have a significant impact on the global cereal market due to its massive domestic production of corn, rice, and wheat. Cereals are main sources of food in low-income countries in Africa and Asia, thus, the impact of China on the availability of cereals in these countries will be modest. In other words, China will not have a significant impact on food security in low-income countries, at least in the coming decade. Between 2015 and 2019, China imported 24 million tonnes of cereals a year on average, accounting for 6 percent of cereals in the world market (National Bureau of Statistics [NBS], 2021a). The Organisation for Economic Co-operation and Development (OECD) and FAO predict that the growth of China's cereal imports from 2020 to 2029 will largely keep pace with the production of cereals in the world. By 2029, China will account for 5 percent of world wheat imports, 7 percent of world rice imports, and an insignificant share in the corn market (Organisation for Economic Co-operation and Development [OECD] and FAO, 2020: 125). This will unlikely have much impact on cereal imports of low-income countries in Africa and Asia.

Third, China's growing imports of resource-intensive foods, such as bovine meat, fish, edible oil, milk, and fruits will likely create a competitive market for imports, which in turn bolsters world prices at higher levels. This will affect some middle- and high-income countries that are also the importers of these foods. For example, China may compete with Japan and South Korea for the import of beef and seafood. China's strong consumption of animal products also adds to the volatility of the global food market, rendering it more vulnerable to shocks. The case of African swine flu is an example. The disease decimated pigs in China in 2018–2020, creating a high demand for meat imports and driving up global meat prices (Mason-D'Croz et al., 2020).

Finally, the growing exports from middle- and low-income countries to China provide an opportunity for farmers in these countries to increase income. However, whether this will benefit small farmers and the rural poor depends largely on agrarian structure in exporting countries. If small farmers enjoy secure land rights and play an active role in food exports, they can increase income through China-bound exports. However, if farmland and agricultural resources are controlled by large producers and corporate capital, an increase in exports would not significantly benefit small farmers. The export boom may also intensify rural struggles and accelerate the pace of rural dispossession as corporate capital seeks to control these resources for increased profitability (McMichael, 2012; Vicol and Pritchard, 2021).

4 Is China a Land Grabber? Overseas Agricultural Investment

China launched the strategy of "going out" in 1999, encouraging and supporting Chinese enterprises to invest overseas. The strategy, together with the WTO accession, marked a giant step in the "global rise of China" (So and Chu, 2016). Agriculture was not a priority for overseas investment initially. It was not until 2006 that the Chinese state outlined a preliminary plan for "agricultural going out," which was then included in subsequent policy documents on agriculture, food security, and foreign aid. The 2006 China–Africa Beijing summit also identified agriculture as a priority area for cooperation, including agricultural investment.

China's overseas agricultural investment drew scrutiny in international media during the 2007/2008 food crisis, even though the country had just begun to support agricultural enterprises to expand beyond borders. In the new millennium, agribusiness corporations accelerated land acquisitions in the Global South. Scholars in critical agrarian and food studies call the phenomenon "land grabbing" and argue that it will have pernicious effects on land rights and livelihoods of peasants and small farmers (Borras et al., 2011; McMichael, 2012; Hall, 2013; Nally, 2015). Nongovernmental organizations (NGOs) and the media also reported extensively on land grabs and suggested that it would undermine food security and sovereignty of low-income countries in Africa and Asia. China was singled out as a leading land grabber in this global land rush. GRAIN, a Europe-based NGO, published a report in 2008 to suggest that China, along with others, was outsourcing domestic food production by purchasing and controlling farms in other countries (GRAIN, 2008). China's alleged land grabs in sub-Saharan Africa particularly unsettled nerves, as the continent was the most food-insecure region in the world. Sensational headlines suggested that the Chinese bought up millions of hectares in Africa and grew food crops for export to China. Similar stories were also featured in media reports in Latin America and Asia (sources cited in Hofman and Ho, 2012; Bräutigam, 2015; Oliveira, 2018).

The literature in the early 2010s revolved around the debate on whether China was a leading land grabber. Empirical studies found that China's role in the global land rush was grossly exaggerated, though the country did invest in farmland in dozens of countries. Deborah Bräutigam and her colleagues conducted extensive field research in Africa and their findings revealed that Chinese enterprises had not acquired large areas of land on the continent (Bräutigam and Ekman, 2012; Bräutigam, 2015). Contrary to the reports that China had seized millions of hectares, their data show that Chinese companies acquired about 100,000 hectares in Africa between 2006 and 2014, and most of the land was either used to grow food crops for local populations or grow cash crops for export to the global market (not necessarily to China), such as rubber and sugarcane (Bräutigam, 2015: 166–168). Empirical studies in Latin America and Southeast Asia also found that Chinese companies acquired much smaller areas of land than reported and that many intended land projects either failed or were drastically scaled back due to local resistance (Chheang, 2017; Oliveira, 2018; Lu and Schönweger, 2019; Mora, 2022). Most of the projects did not target food crops but profitable flex crops, such as palm oil and rubber, and food exports to China from land farmed by Chinese companies were nearly negligible in total food exports to the country (Chen et al., 2017).

This section examines emerging patterns of Chinese overseas agricultural investment. While acquiring use rights of farmland remains a target, the Chinese state and companies have shifted their emphasis away from agriculture to investments in all segments of the supply chains, such as logistics, processing, warehousing, finance, and R&D. These investments aim to increase the country's ability to control supply chains, influence pricing to its advantage, and stimulate agricultural production in exporting countries. In the following, Subsection 4.1 describes the general patterns of Chinese overseas agricultural investment, followed by the analyses of land acquisitions and new directions of investment (Subsections 4.2 and 4.3). Subsection 4.4 discusses theoretical and practical implications.

4.1 Patterns of China's Overseas Agricultural Investment

China's agricultural outward direct investment (ODI) grew rapidly after the launching of the going out strategy. The annual ODI flow increased from

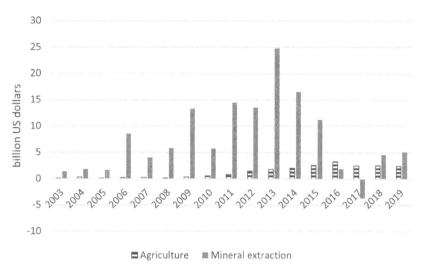

Figure 4 Chinese overseas investment in agriculture and mineral extraction: 2003–2019[20]

US$0.1 billion in 2003 to US$3.3 billion in 2016, before it declined to 2.4 billion in 2019. Agricultural ODI capital stock reached US$19.7 billion in 2019. Despite the rapid growth, agriculture accounts for a very small share of Chinese overseas investment. In 2019, agriculture made up 1.8 percent of all Chinese ODI flow and 0.9 percent of capital stock. The comparison with mineral extraction is striking. Between 2003 and 2019, the flow of agricultural ODI was US$1.3 billion a year on average, whereas that for mineral extraction was US$7.7 billion. Capital stock in mineral extraction, US$175.4 billion by 2019, was also much larger than that in agriculture, US$19.7 billion (Figure 4; National Bureau of Statistics [NBS], 2020). This indicates that Chinese overseas investment has been oriented much more to gaining access to mineral rather than agricultural resources. Mineral extraction generates higher returns for Chinese enterprises and the Chinese state also hopes to gain long-term access to overseas mineral resources for the growth of the Chinese economy (Lee, 2017). Even in the case of agriculture, much of China's overseas investment was also aimed to make profits rather than for food supply.

The Ministry of Agriculture and Rural Affairs of China (MOARA) has conducted comprehensive annual surveys of Chinese companies that invested in agriculture overseas since 2013. The ministry's data show that the number of such enterprises totalled 888 in 2018, investing in 102 countries. Crop farming accounted for 52.2 percent of total agricultural investment

---

[20] Data is derived from the National Bureau of Statistics (NBS) (2021a).

(measured by capital stock), animal husbandry 12.3 percent, forestry 4.4 percent, fishery 4.2 percent, agricultural inputs 1.4 percent, and others (including processing, warehousing, marketing, logistics, and R&D) 25.5 percent (Ministry of Agriculture and Rural Affairs [MOARA], 2019: 3–5). Of crop farming, about half of the investment went to grain crops, while the other half was invested in nongrain crops. The investment in grain crops mainly targeted feed grain such as corn and soybeans, and the main nongrain corps for investment included rubber, sugarcane, palm oil, and cotton. Thus, overall, about a quarter of Chinese overseas agricultural investment was dedicated to grain crops. Chinese enterprises produced 1.8 million tonnes of grain (mainly corn, soybeans, rice, and wheat) overseas in 2018, and this number appears puny in comparison with the country's grain production and grain imports in the same year, 658 million and 109 million, respectively. Furthermore, most of the grain produced in Africa and Latin America were not imported to China but sold in the local market or exported to other countries (Goetz, 2015; Myers and Guo, 2015). Thus, overseas investment in crop production has so far played a negligible role in China's food security.

Geographically, China's agricultural ODI concentrates in Asia and Europe, whereas only a very small proportion has gone to Africa. By 2018, measured by capital stock, 38.3 percent of Chinese agricultural ODI was invested in Asia, much higher than that in Africa: 6.2 percent. The top ten recipients of Chinese agricultural ODI, measured by capital stock, and their shares are as follows: Switzerland (23.1 percent), Australia (7.8 percent), Indonesia (7.4 percent), Laos (7.2 percent), Israel (6.9 percent), New Zealand (5.0 percent), Russia (4.9 percent), France (4.1 percent), Brazil (3.4 percent), and Myanmar (2.8 percent). Chinese companies usually invest in sectors where the recipient countries have comparative advantage or are major exporters of relevant commodities. For example, Chinese companies in Indonesia and Malaysia have targeted palm oil, while those in Myanmar, Laos, and Cambodia grow rice and corn, in additional to commercial crops such as rubber and sugarcane. In Central Asian countries and Russia, Chinese companies have grown wheat, corn, and soybeans. Chinese investment has also targeted meat and dairy sectors in Oceania and Europe and soybeans in South America. In Africa, although Chinese companies have invested in grain crops, much of the investment has also gone to profitable commercial crops and fishery (Ministry of Agriculture and Rural Affairs [MOARA], 2019).

This analysis reveals that Chinese overseas agricultural investment has been oriented more toward making profits than gaining access to agricultural resources for China's food security. Of the 888 enterprises that invested in agriculture overseas in 2018, 814 are private enterprises, and they were responsible for 58 percent of capital stock in China's overseas agricultural ODI (Ministry of Agriculture and Rural Affairs [MOARA], 2019). These enterprises may claim that their investment is for food security at home, for the purpose of seeking loans or subsidies from the Chinese state, but their actual actions are more determined by the profitability of investment.

It should be noted that Chinese overseas agricultural investment is subject to geopolitical relations between China and recipient countries. China's agricultural ODI has mostly gone to the countries with which China has maintained good diplomatic relations. For example, Chinese companies have increased investment in Myanmar, Laos, and Cambodia, whereas much less investment has been made in Vietnam, even though the latter is also a country with rich agricultural resources. Chinese companies have also increased investment in Central Asian countries and Russia, based on the diplomatic platform of the Shanghai Cooperation Organization. In Europe, Chinese agricultural companies have gained a notable presence in Switzerland after the two countries signed a free trade agreement in 2013. When diplomatic relations deteriorate, however, agricultural investment bears the brunt. For instance, Chinese agricultural ODI to Australia had grown rapidly after 2010, and Australia ranked second in terms of capital stock in 2018. However, agricultural ODI from China plummeted in 2018–2019 after the tensions between the two countries flared up (Rowley, 2020; Böhme, 2021). Chinese agricultural investment has made little headway in the United States after the high-profile case of the acquisition of the Smithfield Foods by China's Shuanghui International in 2013. North America accounted for only 1.3 percent of Chinese agricultural ODI capital stock in 2018. The current rivalry between the two countries makes it extremely unlikely that Chinese companies will invest on a large scale in agriculture in the United States in the near future.

4.2 The Chinese Case of "Land Grabbing"

Chinese companies have engaged in a growing number of overseas land deals for agriculture in the past two decades. A Land Matrix report in 2016 ranked China the eighth largest investor country, with approximately 1 million hectares under contract (Nolte et al., 2016). The top five investor countries were Malaysia, the United States, the United Kingdom, Singapore, and Saudi Arabia. While the Land Matrix has built probably the most comprehensive database on land deals in the Global South and Eastern Europe, its data collection has largely relied on media reports and company statements, some of which are impossible to verify. This limitation is acknowledged in the Land Matrix's reports and website.

The Land Matrix database records Chinese land deals in Asia, Eastern Europe, Africa, and South America. The latest updated database records 104 Chinese concluded land deals with agricultural intention between 2000 and 2021.[21] Chinese enterprises acquired 2.1 million hectares from host countries through these land deals, accounting for 9 percent of such lands by all investor countries recorded in the database. Most of the lands were acquired by lease (full-use rights for a limited number of years) or with concession (partial-use rights for a limited number of years), whereas only 43,000 hectares (2 percent of the total) were acquired through outright purchases. Of the total acquired land area, 461,000 hectares, or 22 percent of the total, are intended for food crops, whereas more than 1 million hectares are intended for biofuels or nonfood agricultural commodities, and the rest is either intended for livestock or unspecified purposes. The data again show that Chinese investment has been directed more toward profitable commercial agriculture than food production. Asia accounts for the largest share of the land area acquired, covering about 1.4 million hectares and accounting for 68.2 percent (Table 4). Within Asia, the top target countries are Myanmar, Laos, and Cambodia, and these three countries account for nearly 90 percent of the land area that Chinese enterprises acquired in Asia. In Eastern Europe, Chinese land deals are concentrated in Russia and Belarus, and Russia alone has leased 233,000 hectares to Chinese companies. The data again show that Africa is not a primary target for Chinese agricultural investment in land. The continent accounts for 8 percent of the land acquired by Chinese enterprises. Chinese land deals are also minuscule in South America despite the continent's abundant land resources. The top three target countries are Venezuela, Jamaica, and Brazil, from which Chinese companies acquired 60,000, 18,000, and 16,000 hectares, respectively.

The Land Matrix database has not recorded Chinese land deals in Central Asia and Oceania, and research shows that there are Chinese investments in agricultural land there (Hofman, 2016; Böhme, 2021). However, the database may also overreport the number of effective land deals and land area of acquisition. This is because land deals usually catch news when they are signed, but there is insufficient information regarding whether and when the land projects go into operation. Of the 104 land deals, 56 are marked "in operation," whereas there is no information on the implementation status of 34 deals in the database, and 14 deals have not started or started without any production. In other words, the Land Matrix can only verify that about half of the deals have

---

[21] The number excludes forestry projects and the projects that have been abandoned. The data were retrieved from the website https://landmatrix.org.

Table 4 Chinese land deals with agricultural intention in the Land Matrix database

	Asia	Eastern Europe	Africa	South America	Total
Number of land deals	61	11	25	7	104
Land area (1,000 hectares)	1,396	363	165	125	2,049
Share in total land area (%)	68.2	17.7	8.0	6.1	100.0
Top target countries (land area, 1,000 hectares)	Myanmar (808) Laos (330) Cambodia (116)	Russia (233) Belarus (100)	Cameroon (45) Mozambique (45) Madagascar (24)	Venezuela (60) Jamaica (18) Brazil (16)	

entered the production phase. The verified land area that is in production amounts to 248,000 hectares, only 12.1 percent of the total.

Empirical studies based on field research reveal that overseas Chinese agricultural projects often operate on a scale much smaller than the land area granted in the contract. Southeast Asia accounts for the largest share of Chinese investments in land in the Land Matrix database. Chheang (2017) shows that thirty Chinese projects invested in the agri-food industry in Cambodia, covering 237,406 hectares of land. Although twenty-one projects were in operation, only about 42,081 hectares were cultivated. Lu and Schönweger (2019) studied seven Chinese agribusiness investments in Laos and found that the amount of land actually allocated to Chinese companies was significantly smaller than the areas granted by the Laos state. Kenney-Lazar's (2018) investigation also found that Chinese investors in Laos were not able to fully acquire the land granted to them due to the resistance of rural residents and civil society actors. However, it should be noted that small-scale land acquisitions may have significant implications on local livelihoods. Friis and Nielsen (2016) documented a case of two Chinese investors leasing land from villagers in northern Laos to grow bananas. Although the villagers received rent for the concession, the land use change had resulted in the destruction of field structures and irrigation systems, and heavy chemical use also caused environmental degradation, which would negatively affect rural livelihoods in the long term.

In Latin America, Chinese land deals often failed to follow through or were much smaller than reported in the media. While NGOs and the media claimed that Chinese companies acquired 800,000 hectares in Latin America, Myers and Guo (2015) confirmed that only 70,000 hectares were leased by Chinese companies for crop cultivation. The authors found that Chinese land investment in Venezuela amounted to only 3,500 hectares and that the 60,000-hectare land deal by China's Beidahuang Group, also recorded in the Land Matrix database, could not be verified. Oliveira (2018) conducted field research in Brazil and could only confirm relatively small-scale land deals by Chinese investors, amounting to 68,600 hectares, in contrast to millions of hectares reported in the media. Furthermore, all land investments were in trouble, and some lands were left fallow due to economic losses. Despite their nonexistence or failure, alleged large land deals by Chinese companies have triggered fear and anxiety in Latin America, leading to restrictive legislation over foreign acquisitions of agricultural lands in Brazil, Argentina, and other countries (Myers and Guo, 2015; Oliveira, 2018; Søndergaard, 2020; Mora, 2022).

In Central Asia and Eastern Europe, Russia has been the largest recipient of Chinese investment for crop production. There are reports that small Chinese farmers have leased farms or worked as farmworkers in the Russian Far East since the 1990s. In the last two decades, agricultural companies have started to lease land in the area and grow corn and soybeans (Zhou, 2016). By 2018, there were seventy-eight agricultural companies investing in Russia, and twenty-three of them engaged in crop production (Ministry of Agriculture and Rural Affairs [MOARA], 2019: 30). Agricultural companies in Central Asia and Russia produced about 1 million tonnes of soybeans and cereals in 2018, most of which were grown in Russia. Although crop production is for the Chinese market, the export of crop products is controlled by Russia. In 2017, Russia imposed restrictions on farmland leasing and land use by foreign companies and legislated that all crops grown by foreign investors must be exported through Russian companies (Lu, 2020). My fieldwork in Heilongjiang in July 2019, the Chinese province bordering Russia, revealed that Chinese companies investing in Russia faced restrictions in exporting crops back to China. In Central Asian countries, such as Kazakhstan and Tajikistan, the lands leased by Chinese companies or farmers are usually small, and much of the production has so far been intended for the local market. Nevertheless, both Kazakhstan and Tajikistan imposed restrictions on farmland leasing by foreign investors, mainly in response to the growing investment from China (Hofman, 2016; Bitabarova, 2018).

The previous analysis reveals that Chinese overseas investments in farmland have faced many hurdles. Most of high-profile large land deals, highlighted in the media or NGO reports, did not materialize. Host countries have imposed various restrictions on these investments, in response to the discourse of the "Chinese threat." Most Chinese farmland acquisitions took place in neighboring countries such as Laos, Myanmar, and Russia, and land acquisitions in Africa and South America are much smaller than reported. In addition, the literature on land grabbing is vague in defining "land grabs." The term indicates coercion, forceful seizure of land assets, and dispossession of small holders, but most studies regard all land deals as land grabs even though these deals do not meet those conditions. Some Chinese land investments in Africa, Southeast Asia, and Latin America were initiated in the form of agricultural aid or cooperation in order to stimulate domestic agricultural production for local needs, but they are also indistinguishably counted as Chinese land acquisitions overseas (Yan and Sautman, 2010; Myers and Guo, 2015; Lawther, 2017; Zhan et al., 2018).

The Chinese experience of investing in agricultural land overseas suggests the crucial difference between China and the nineteenth-century British Empire in shaping the global food system. While China has increasingly relied on food resources beyond borders to feed its population, the country is unable to exert direct control of agricultural lands in other countries. With more and more Chinese companies investing in agriculture overseas, studies find that Chinese companies, like multinational agribusiness companies from other countries, prioritize biofuels and commercial crops for profits, and attempt to circumvent environmental regulations and avoid corporate responsibilities (Goetz, 2015; Myers and Guo, 2015; Chen et al., 2017; Oliveira et al., 2021). However, these issues should not be equated with the direct control of overseas agricultural resources by China. After investigating Chinese investments in rural Africa, Deborah Bräutigam concluded,

> There is no evidence to support the notion that Chinese firms in rural Africa are the beachhead of a rising imperial power. Rather, they are part of a new wave of globalization that began in the 1980s ... Chinese companies are at the start of their learning curve as global businesses. But the rules these companies play by and the corporate social responsibility issue their investments raise are very different from the military conquests and political domination that occurred in the 19th century. No Chinese in Africa plays a role remotely like that played the English businessman and financier Cecil Rhodes or Belgium's King Leopold. (2015: 163)

4.3 New Directions in China's Overseas Agricultural Investment

Over the past decade, China has deemphasized the narrow focus on agricultural production and instead stressed the investment in the "whole supply chain" (全产业链), which comprises the supply of agricultural inputs, infrastructure development (e.g., irrigation), farming, processing, warehousing, trading, logistics, and R&D. The goal is to strengthen the infrastructure of supply chains, mitigate the risk of import disruption, influence the pricing of agri-food commodities, and increase returns by engaging in higher value-added business functions. According to MOARA, by 2018, 27 percent of overseas agricultural investment, or US$5.3 billion, was invested in agricultural inputs or activities other than production (Ministry of Agriculture and Rural Affairs [MOARA], 2019: 38). However, this figure excludes the mergers and acquisitions (M&As), which have become a major target of Chinese agriculture-related investment overseas.

Between 2010 and 2018, Chinese companies invested US$69 billion in agriculture-related M&As overseas (Ministry of Agriculture and Rural Affairs [MOARA], 2020b), much higher than agricultural ODI capital stock – US$19.7 billion. Some large M&As by Chinese agribusiness companies captured media headlines. It was widely reported when Shuanghui International (the WH Group) acquired the United States's Smithfield Foods for US$4.7 billion in 2013. In 2016, ChemChina acquired Syngenta for US$43 billion, the largest acquisition ever by a Chinese company. Mergers and acquisitions allow

Chinese companies to expand into strategic, higher value-added business functions in the value chains. For instance, China National Cereals, Oils and Foodstuffs Corporation (COFCO), the most prominent state-owned Chinese company in agriculture and commodity trading, acquired Nidera and Noble Agri in 2014-2016 for a combined total of US$2.8 billion. Nidera and Noble Agri are large global agribusiness companies in grain trading and processing. The two acquisitions allow COFCO to own agricultural assets in twenty-six countries, including those in Latin America and Eastern Europe, and most of these assets are logistics and transportation facilities, processing centers, and trading marketplaces (Gooch and Gale, 2018). Mergers and acquisitions have also been used to increase overseas market shares, source the supply of food materials, and extend business functions forward or backward along the supply chain. Bright Foods, a Shanghai-based Chinese company, acquired companies in dairy and meat sectors in Oceania and Europe to supply such products to the Chinese market (Gooch and Gale, 2018: 36).

It should be noted that M&As by Chinese agribusiness companies are part of the global trend of consolidation among agri-food and biochemical companies as the capitalist agri-food economy has been transformed into an increasingly oligopolistic structure and as financial interests of agri-food capital trump the interests of producers and consumers (Clapp, 2014). Besides the acquisition of Syngenta by ChemChina, Dow and Du Pont announced a merger deal of US$13 billion in 2015, while Monsanto was acquired by Bayer for US$66 billion in 2016. The justifications for these M&As are "efficiency and enhanced shareholder value," but the control of the markets of seeds and agricultural inputs by these giant conglomerates leaves growers and consumers much fewer options, and the enhanced use of biochemicals and genetic-engineering technologies in agriculture is likely to further damage environment and food security (Patel, 2012; Bratspies, 2017).

The involvement of Chinese companies in global agri-food M&As has not always been successful. Not only were some M&As by Chinese companies seen as a threat and rejected by host countries, the operation of global businesses after the M&As often ran into difficulty. For example, Nidera experienced large losses after COFCO's acquisition, and Shuanghui International had difficulty in paying the loan for the acquisition of Smithfield Foods (Gooch and Gale, 2018: 42). More recently, the acquisition of Syngenta has left ChemChina to struggle with a "debt mountain" and suffer large losses (Lu et al., 2020), and the acquisition would also likely create another oligopolistic company in the Chinese market of agricultural inputs at the expense of small enterprises and farmers. The acquisition was such a risky deal that Mr. Geng Wenbing, the Chinese ambassador to Switzerland (2016–2020), remarked in 2019 that the deal would not occur if he had been appointed the ambassador one year earlier (Bosley, 2019).

Another new direction is the alignment of "agricultural going out" with the BRI. The BRI project, launched in 2013, is a grand Chinese strategy to promote investment in and trade with countries in Asia, Africa, and Europe. The Chinese government has identified agriculture as a major area for bilateral and multilateral cooperation under the initiative (China National Development and Reform Commission [NDRC], 2015). In May 2017, the Ministry of Agriculture (MOA)[22] and Ministry of Foreign Affairs, together with others, released a document entitled *Vision and Action on Jointly Promoting Agricultural Cooperation on the Belt and Road* (Ministry of Agriculture of China [MOA], 2017), which serves as a guideline for Chinese agricultural engagement in the BRI countries. The document highlights the need to increase the investment in agricultural infrastructure, processing, warehousing, logistics, and R&D. It also laid out a plan to build "overseas demonstration parks" for agricultural cooperation, which is to integrate the whole supply chain, increase agricultural productivity, promote R&D and manpower training, and build trade infrastructure.

In 2017, MOA identified the first ten overseas demonstration parks in BRI countries: Tajikistan, Kyrgyzstan, Sudan, Mozambique, Tanzania, Uganda, Zambia, Cambodia, Laos, and Fiji. These demonstration parks are based on existing Chinese agricultural investments or agricultural cooperation projects between China and the host country. In these parks, the Chinese agribusiness companies have leased land from the host country and built infrastructure, processing factories, R&D centers, and other facilities. The guideline document suggests that the Chinese state would provide financial loans and subsidies for these companies to improve or expand their projects so that the demonstration parks will draw in other Chinese companies or non-Chinese companies, and as a result, their businesses together would cover more segments in the whole supply chain. According to the bilateral agricultural agreements, the host countries are usually required to approve land concessions, build supporting infrastructure, and provide policy support for Chinese investments in these demonstration parks.[23]

By 2018, the BRI countries accounted for 47 percent of Chinese agricultural ODI capital stock (Ministry of Agriculture and Rural Affairs [MOARA], 2019: 34). Some of the largest recipient countries of Chinese agricultural ODI have joined the BRI, including Laos, Myanmar, Cambodia, Indonesia, and Russia.

---

[22] The ministry was renamed the Ministry of Agriculture and Rural Affairs (MOARA) in March 2018.

[23] The introductions of these demonstration parks are available at the website of the China Council for the Promotion of International Trade (https://oip.ccpit.org).

The promotion of the BRI project will further increase agricultural investment in these countries. The BRI project, if successful, will serve China's global food strategy. First, trade and investment under the project will diversify importer countries and create new suppliers of food imports. The volume of food trade between China and BRI countries in Southeast Asia, Central Asia, and Eastern Europe has markedly increased since the launch of the project (Zhan et al., 2018). These countries supply China with both rich-diet foods, such as meat, milk, seafood, and fruits, and grain, including wheat, corn, and rice. Cambodia, Laos, and Myanmar have become new sources of rice and corn imports for China, while Central Asian countries, Russia, and Ukraine have increased their shares in China's imports of corn, wheat, and soybeans (Table 2).

Second, BRI countries provide a platform for Chinese agricultural companies to learn and grow into global businesses. As noted earlier, not all overseas investments of Chinese companies are aimed to increase the import of agri-food resources to China. An equally important goal is to enhance the competitiveness of these companies in the global food economy and increase their share in the global market. Many Chinese companies invest overseas to boost the export of their products and services to the host country or a third country. The Chinese state also encourages these activities as they will increase the influence and positioning of Chinese companies in the global supply chains, which in turn could lead to the greater control of these chains.

Last, the deepening of food relations with the BRI countries could create alternate food trade routes and mitigate the risk of trade disruption, particularly the disruption of food imports to China. The BRI project envisions to establish six economic corridors (Table 5), and these corridors, if successfully built, will create trade routes that bypass major chokepoints such as the Suez Canal and the Straits of Malacca (Tortajada and Zhang, 2021). This undoubtedly serves China's geopolitical interests, as China has long been concerned about the potential cut-off of the supply of raw materials and food products to the country. This concern has only intensified in the context of US–China rivalry and the possible occurrence of a new cold war.

4.4 Summary and Assessment

Over the past two decades, Chinese overseas agricultural investment has grown rapidly, but it still accounts for a very small proportion of all overseas investment by Chinese companies. Nevertheless, Chinese agricultural companies have gained a notable presence in overseas agricultural deals and M&As, and they engaged in a wide range of activities besides crop production. China was once depicted as a leading land grabber, but this section shows that Chinese

Table 5 Six economic corridors under the BRI

	Corridor	Connecting countries/regions
1	China–Mongolia–Russia Corridor	China, Russia, and Mongolia
2	New Eurasian Land Bridge	More than thirty countries and regions in Eurasia, from China to the Netherlands and Belgium
3	China–Central Asia–West Asia Corridor	Five countries in Central Asia and seventeen countries in West Asia
4	China–Pakistan Corridor	Countries in South and Central Asia, North Africa, and along the Persian Gulf
5	Bangladesh–China–Myanmar Corridor	Southeast Asia and South Asia
6	China–Indochina Peninsula Corridor	Southeast Asia

companies have only engaged in a modest number of land deals, significant but far from a leading country of land acquisitions. Furthermore, their land deals were often restricted and resisted in the host country, and many land-based investments ran into difficulty or incurred large losses. During the last decade, the Chinese state has deemphasized the focus on crop production and land investment and instead encouraged the investments in the whole supply chain to safeguard food imports to the country. Overseas agricultural investment has also been aligned with the BRI, which could build alternative food trade routes to China.

The survey of Chinese overseas agricultural investment challenges some conventional assumptions in the literature. First, the land grabbing literature argues that a primary motive of foreign land acquisitions is to control agricultural resources for food security, but the Chinese case demonstrates that most of the land investments are for profit rather than for food. As noted earlier, although Chinese companies have acquired a significant number of farmlands overseas, the crop output from these farmlands appears negligible compared with the country's domestic production and food imports. Furthermore, foreign land acquisitions might not be an effective way to secure resources for food security, which can be easily subject to local resistance and export bans in times of crisis. The Chinese state has become fully aware of this constraint as the country's overseas investments have often been subject to restrictions (Chen, 2012). The Chinese case probably holds true for other land-scare, capital-rich Asian countries as well. Take Singapore as an example. The city-state was ranked the fourth in overseas land acquisitions in the 2016 Land Matrix report (Nolte et al., 2016). With a population of only 5.7 million, the country would feel a strong sense of food security due to its large-scale overseas land acquisitions. However, the city-state has increasingly worried about the disruption of food supply from overseas in the past decade, and in 2019, it set a goal to produce 30 percent of its food by 2030, up from 10 percent (Chang, 2019). Many other countries have also implemented policies to increase the ratio of food self-sufficiency after the 2007/2008 food crisis (Clapp, 2017).

Second, the food regime literature tends to draw a historical analogy between China and the British Empire as they either transformed or could transform the global food system as major food importers, but the failures of and resistance to Chinese agricultural investment, particularly land acquisitions, reveal China's precarious position in seeking direct control of overseas agricultural resources. This forces the country to search for alternative means of control as well as support domestic production. In other words, new directions of Chinese agricultural investment not only reflect a reorientation of China's global food strategy but also the vulnerability of the country in seeking overseas agricultural resources. This vulnerability suggests that China's role in the international agri-food order in the future would be fundamentally different from that of the British Empire in the late nineteenth and early twentieth centuries, the period of the first food regime conceptualized by Friedmann and McMichael (1989). Based on the analyses in Sections 2 and 3, we could surmise that China would reshape the international agri-food order in the twenty-first century by the following measures:

- import diversification; the cultivation of good diplomatic relations with countries in Asia, Africa, and South America;
- overseas agricultural investments to reduce food import competitors and increase the production capacity of exporting countries;
- the establishment of multiple alternative food trade routes; direct or indirect control of production and trade infrastructures;
- and the diffusion of agricultural science and technology to boost crop production in China and beyond.

Third, the resource-extraction literature rarely distinguishes between food and other raw materials such as minerals (Veltmeyer, 2013), but the case of China shows notable differences between them. Not only has the scale of agricultural investment from China been much smaller than that of mineral extraction, but investment in crop production must take into account the needs of the host country before food products can be exported to China. This is for both economic and geopolitical reasons. Economically, China hopes to reduce competitors for food imports and increase the global supply of food. Geopolitically, agricultural cooperation and food aid are important means for China to cultivate diplomatic relations in the Global South. Hence, China is reluctant to import foods, particularly staple foods, from countries that are experiencing food shortages. According to Du Ying, the former Deputy Director of the China National Development and Reform Commission (NDRC) and a prominent official expert on China's food security, China must produce enough cereals because there are only about 300 million tonnes of cereals traded in the global market every year, half of China's annual consumption. If China imported too much staple food, it would lead to dramatic price hikes in the global market. It is not only too costly for China, but it would also negatively affect China's relations with developing countries, where there are still more than 800 million people in hunger (Du and Han, 2020).

This section has shown that encouraging and supporting agribusiness companies to invest overseas constitutes an integral component of China's global food strategy. The Chinese state has decided to achieve food security by supporting agrarian capital and build an alliance with agribusiness companies, both state-owned and private. However, there are tensions between the interests of Chinese companies and the state's goals. As noted earlier, the motivation for profit clearly overrides the goal of food security when Chinese companies invest in agriculture overseas. It remains a question whether Chinese companies would sacrifice the profit-making goal when they invest in processing, warehousing, logistics, and R&D, particularly when profit-making conflicts with the long-term goal of food security. The next section scrutinizes state-capital relations in the country's food security strategy, particularly the efforts to support and build large agribusiness companies, both at home and overseas.

5 In the Name of Food Security: State-Led Capitalism and Agribusiness Expansion

The exports of Chinese textiles to the US market grew rapidly after China's accession to the WTO. Concerned about job losses and trade deficits, the United States imposed quotas to limit textile imports from China in November 2003 (Andrews, 2003). This unsettled the Chinese leadership as the textile industry accounted for 20 percent of the country's total exports at the time, and the US policy would also set an example for others such as EU to follow. To avoid further escalation of trade tensions, a Chinese delegation of senior officials and prominent entrepreneurs, led by the Premier, made an official visit to the United States in December 2003 and offered to purchase large quantities of US commodities. The soybean was on the list. Chinese companies initially pledged to purchase

5 million tonnes of soybeans, and later signalled the intention to purchase another 5 million tonnes. The large purchases excited soybean traders on the Chicago Board of Trade, and the rumor that the soybean yield in the United States would decline caused soybean prices to soar in the futures market. Consequently, Chinese companies agreed to abnormally high prices. After the deals were signed, however, soybean prices dropped. It was estimated that Chinese companies overpaid at least US$1.5 billion for the purchases (Oliveira and Schneider, 2016: 178). The huge financial losses caused 70 percent of soybean oil crushing facilities in China to go bankrupt or cease production. Sensing the opportunities created by Chinese companies' financial troubles, international grain traders and agribusinesses, including the agribusiness giants ABCD, moved to merge and acquire Chinese oil crushing companies. By 2007, foreign agribusiness companies increased their share in the Chinese oil crushing industry to 48 percent, up from 9 percent in 2000. In addition, the ABCD controlled 80 percent of China's soybean imports (Grainwiz, 2009; Wang, 2013: 96).

This was known as the "soybean debacle" (大豆沦陷) in China. The crisis sent shockwaves through the Chinese soybean industry and startled the central authority. It was widely believed that the upheaval of soybean prices was manipulated. The Chinese central government attributed the crisis to the country's inability to foresee and control the fluctuations of commodity prices in the global market (Zang, 2013: 20–30). Despite being the largest importer of soybeans in the world, China must rely on the ABCD group to import most of its soybeans. To increase the control of soybean imports and the oil crushing industry, the Chinese state issued a policy in August 2008 to support the creation of China's own global agribusiness companies, which could control the supply chain of the soybean industry and have the price-setting capability in the global market (China National Development and Reform Commission [NDRC], 2008). The China National Cereals, Oils and Foodstuffs Corporation was chosen for this ambition. The state-owned enterprise (SOE) was urged to sign deals directly with overseas soybean producers, lease ports, construct warehouses and logistic facilities, establish soybean processing factories, and form joint ventures with local companies in exporting countries. Thereafter, creating global agribusinesses has become a key component of China's global food strategy, with the aim of safeguarding the overseas supply of food to China.

The Chinese efforts to create global agribusinesses have led scholars to employ terms such as "state capitalism," "state-led capitalism," "agro-security mercantilism," and "neomercantilism" to characterize a new model in sourcing and controlling overseas agri-food resources (McMichael, 2013, 2020; Belesky and Lawrence, 2019). According to Philip McMichael, agro-security mercantilism refers to a new form of mercantilism in which states initiate "acquisition of (or access to) land offshore to circumvent extant markets and intermediaries to guarantee supplies of food, feed and fuel" (2020: 121). This is in response to the triple cries (financial, energy, and food) in the new millennium, which have intensified the concern over access to offshore agri-food resources (McMichael, 2013). China's support for SOEs overseas M&As, the going out strategy, and the BRI project are all taken as evidence that the country has been practicing neomercantilism. However, McMichael is inconclusive on whether neomercantilism prefigures the emergence of a new system different from the corporate food regime, as he notes that agro-security mercantilism "both affirms and contradicts a neoliberal order" (McMichael, 2013: 47). Belesky and Lawrence (2019) also note that "mercantilism has played a constitutive role in the evolution of various food regimes" in history (2019: 8) and that China's state capitalism and neomercantilism are "both challenging and co-constituting the neoliberal characteristics of the contemporary food regime in transition" (2019: 11).

The case of the soybean crisis also suggests that China does not intend to challenge the neoliberal order of the global food system. The support for Chinese global agribusinesses following the crisis is mainly to increase the control of overseas food supply. Furthermore, China is interested in maintaining the neoliberal food system as it has benefited from it. The accession to the WTO allows the country to import large volumes of foods from the global market, while the overseas expansion of Chinese agribusiness companies has been made possible by the deregulation of offshore investment and the free movement of financial capital across borders.

This section focuses on state-capital alliance in China's agri-food sectors. The alliance has grown out of the concern for national food security and contributed to the rapid expansion of Chinese agribusinesses both at home and abroad, but the pursuit of profit has often made the claim on food security dubious. Although China's state-led capitalism and agribusiness expansion are not aimed to undermine the neoliberal order, its actions may induce the structural change of the global food system. It would further undermine the dominance of northern countries and give rise to a multipolar global food system, with China emerging as a key pole (Belesky and Lawrence, 2019). In addition, the global expansion of Chinese agribusinesses will intensify corporate competition, leading to the further penetration of corporate capital into food commodity frontiers. There has been a growing body of scholarship on China's support for the global expansion of its agribusinesses. This section contributes to the literature by highlighting the domestic origin of such state-capital alliance.

5.1 Dragonheads and New Units of Operation

Rural reform in 1978 spurred rapid rural growth and raised China's grain production to a new height in the 1980s, but the trend did not last. In the 1990s, the Chinese countryside had descended into a crisis: rural economic growth was far outpaced by a rapidly expanding urban economy, peasants left the village in desperation for any jobs in the city, and farmland was left uncultivated or undercultivated. The rural crisis should be, at least partly, attributed to urban bias policies at the time, such as the frenzy to build economic development zones, the rapid upgrading of urban infrastructure, and favorable land use and tax policies for urban industries (Hsing, 2010; Zhan, 2019a: 61–78). Scholars and policy makers who promote the modernist discourse, however, blame smallholder farming for the rural crisis. In the 1990s, China's agricultural land was cultivated by rural households of more than 200 million, and each household farmed only half a hectare on average. The modernist discourse perceives small household farms as backward, weak, and scattered, and suggests that they should be replaced by large, modern farms (Zhang and Donaldson, 2008; Schneider, 2015).

Despite the growth in grain production from 1995 to 1997, the Chinese state decided to introduce large agrarian capital to agriculture. In October 1998, the CCP Central Committee released a guideline document titled "Decision of the CCP Central Committee on Major Issues Concerning Agriculture and Rural Areas" (*Xinhua* 1998), which includes plans to promote future agricultural development through agricultural industrialization (农业产业化). The document also specifies that a major means to achieve agricultural industrialization is to nurture and support agribusiness companies.

The initial strategy was not to replace small household farms with agribusiness companies and large farms; rather, the Chinese state encouraged the cooperation between them, with agribusiness companies integrating farming households in the form of contract farming. Thus, agribusiness companies in China are called "dragonhead companies" (龙头企业), suggesting that they should work with and bring along farming households, which constitute the dragon's body. The number of dragonhead companies increased rapidly from 27,000 in 2000 to 129,000 in 2016 (Zhan, 2017a). In recent years, such companies decreased in the number (90,000 in 2020), but their scale has grown, with increasing dominance of large agribusiness corporations in the market. In 2020, the central government recognized the largest 1,547 agribusiness companies as "national key dragonheads," which meet the criteria on annual gross sales and net income (Schneider, 2017). Of these dragonheads, the top 100 achieved a combined gross income of 2.3 trillion yuan (US$354 billion) in 2020, 68 percent of the group's total (Ministry of Agriculture and Rural Affairs [MOARA], 2021). In October 2021, MOARA issued a policy document to further support dragonheads to grow larger and stronger. The goal is to nurture more than 2,000 national key dragonheads by 2025.[24] The expansion of dragonheads owes much to state support. The governments at both central and local levels provided subsidies, funds, bank loans, land use quotas, and other supportive measures for these companies (Trappel, 2015; Zhan, 2019a, 92–93). The 2021 document further supports the M&As among dragonheads to build giant agribusiness corporations.

With regard to crop farming, the rural policy shifted after 2008 to nurture the *new units of operation* (新型经营主体), which are much larger than small household farms. The new units of operation include specialized farming households, family farms, and agricultural cooperatives. Later agricultural companies were also added to the list (Zhan, 2017a).[25] By 2020, the numbers of agricultural cooperatives and family farms reached 2.3 million and 3 million, respectively (Li, 2021). The large farming units are created through land transfer: that is, the transfer of farmland from peasants to large farms and agricultural companies. By 2020, 37 million hectares of farmland had been transferred, accounting for more than a third of the total acreage of farmland that was cultivated by rural households. Although it is stipulated that land transfer must be agreed by peasants, local authorities often coerce peasants to transfer land rights in the interest of new units of operation (Ye, 2015; Luo et al., 2017).

5.2 From Domestic Expansion to Global Agribusiness

The policy to support dragonheads spurred the expansion of Chinese agribusiness companies. After the soybean debacle in 2004, such support has been further enhanced, and the measures include the fast-track authorizations of M&As and public listing in the stock exchange, the provision of subsidies, low-interest loans from state-owned banks, and the granting of licenses for international trade. In the first decade of the twenty-first century, Chinese agribusiness companies had yet to become global agribusinesses, though some of them started to invest overseas. During this period, these companies had mostly focused on domestic expansion.

The China National Cereals, Oils and Foodstuffs Corporation, China's largest food processor and commodity trader, is a case in point. Established during the socialist period (1949–1978) to manage China's agricultural exports and imports,

---

[24] The document is in Chinese and can be accessed at www.gov.cn/zhengce/zhengceku/2021-10/27/content_5645191.htm.

[25] Agricultural companies refer to the companies that engage directly in agricultural production, and many of such companies are also agribusiness companies as they are involved in agribusinesses other than agricultural production.

COFCO expanded rapidly during the corporate reforms in the 1990s by establishing dozens of subsidiary companies and acquiring assets of other SOEs. The China National Cereals, Oils and Foodstuffs Corporation was also a pioneer of utilizing financial markets. As early as 1993, the corporation acquired two companies listed in the Hong Kong Stock Exchange, and established COFCO International Limited and Top Glory International Holdings Limited there. Between 1987 and 2004, the value of COFCO's assets grew from 2.5 to 46.6 billion yuan, up seventeen times. After 2004, COFCO embarked on a spree of M&As within China. Within a decade, the corporation acquired more than a dozen large SOEs and private companies. In 2016, COFOC acquired another giant Chinese SOE, the Chinatex Corporation, which owned thirty subsidiaries and forty manufacturing plants, and engaged in the trade and production of textiles, grain, and edible oils. By 2017, the value of COFCO assets reached 539 billion yuan, more than eleven times its asset value in 2004. After these M&As, the corporation expanded its business into a wide range of areas, including but not limited to, grain and edible oils, dairy and meat, animal husbandry, wine and beverages, chemicals, biofuels, logistics and packaging, real estate, and finance. In 2009, the corporation branded its strategy as one controlling "the whole supply chain," from the farm to the dining table, in agri-food sectors, which was later adopted as a national policy to support the global expansion of Chinese agribusiness (Xu et al., 2014; *Xinhua*, 2018b; Zhang, 2018: 249–251; Ren, 2019; China National Cereals, Oils and Foodstuffs Corporation [COFCO], 2021).

Other large Chinese agribusiness corporations experienced similar expansion through M&As in the two decades after the Chinese state pledged support for dragonheads. Zhang (2018: 237–246) classifies potential Chinese global agribusinesses into three categories: central SOEs, state farms, and private dragonhead enterprises. Besides COFCO, another two state-owned agribusiness giants, China National Agricultural Development Group Co. Ltd. (CNADC) and ChemChina had also acquired a number of domestic enterprises before they expanded overseas during the last decade. State farms, such as Beidahuang and Guangdong Nongken, and private dragonheads, such as the WH Group and the New Hope Group, have also followed the path from domestic to overseas expansion.

The rise of large Chinese agribusinesses not only added new players into the global food system but also profoundly altered agri-food sectors in China. The efforts to build giant agribusiness corporations have moved China's agri-food economy toward an oligopolistic structure, evidenced by the decreasing number of small dragonheads and the increasing dominance of giant dragonheads in the past decade. As a result, large agribusiness corporations have exerted growing control over business functions of the supply chain, from production to consumption, including supplying agricultural inputs, food processing, shipping, warehousing, wholesale trading, marketing, finance, R&Ds, and recently, digital marketing through online platforms. This squeezes profit margins for small farmers and small enterprises while driving up commodity prices for consumers. For instance, COFCO, along with a few other large companies, pushed up the consumer prices of edible oil considerably in China from 2010 to 2012 due to their near monopoly of the market (Dai and Zhang, 2012: 6). This makes the Chinese agri-food economy increasingly look like the hourglass structure described by Raj Patel (2012: 19–22): Hundreds of millions of small farmers and consumers are located at the ends of production and consumption, but only a small number of large agribusiness corporations in the middle controlling the supply of food from farms to dining tables. These corporations thus have the power to bend the prices in their favor but at the expense of both small farmers and consumers.

5.3 State-Capital Alliance in the Name of Food Security

The Chinese state entered an alliance with agrarian capital for the sake of food security. Domestically, it believes that agribusiness and large farms are able to produce more grain and food stuffs than small producers. Beyond the borders, it believes that the expansion of Chinese agribusiness corporations such as COFCO increases the control of supply chains and thus protects the stable supply of food to China. Agrarian capital has also responded actively by playing up their role in and commitment to the country's food security, particularly when they need support from the state (Zhan, 2017a; Zhang, 2018: 257). For instance, during the US–China trade war in 2018, COFCO asserted that it would and could seek more soybean imports from South America and Eastern Europe to make up shortfalls in the imports from the United States (Wang, 2018: 5). Whether and to what extent state-capital alliance will improve the country's food security, however, remains to be answered. The following analysis shows that such an alliance does not necessarily contribute to food security at global, national, or household levels.

First, as noted previously, the extent of a "free" global food market is often exaggerated. Although neoliberal discourse and policy since the 1980s pro-moted the free flows of food commodities across borders, this took place when the supply of these commodities generally exceeded the demand, and the major exporters, such as the United States, EU, and NACs, competed to increase their shares in the export market. When food is in tight supply, as happened during the 2007/2008 food crisis and the early phase of the COVID-19 outbreak, the export countries would prioritize domestic needs and impose export embargos. The greater control of trade routes, logistics, and other functions in supply chains would mitigate the bottleneck problem in the logistics of international trade and reduce the costs of transportation, but it helps little when the exporting countries control or prohibit food exports.

The second problem is the tension between profitability and food security. As noted earlier, overseas agricultural investment by Chinese agribusinesses focuses much more on profitable flex crops and activities rather than food crops. The Chinese state also requires that these agribusinesses must make profits when they do business overseas, as it cannot subsize their operations indefinitely. Thus, agribusiness corporations are in a strong position to bargain with the state in their pursuit of profits, and they are able to push up food prices due to their monopoly in the market. These profit-making activities do not always contribute to food security. For instance, COFCO posted a record profit of US $414 million in 2020, but this was achieved in times of high food prices during the COVID-19 pandemic, when food insecurity increased globally (Food and Agriculture Organization of the UN [FAO] et al., 2021). Within China, food prices had also risen considerably, increasing the risk of food insecurity for low-income populations (Mullen, 2021).

The third problem concerns corruption. Although the Chinese state has direct control of the personnel of large state-owned agribusinesses, it faces the difficulty to monitor their managers' corrupt activities, which often undermine national food security. A good example is China Grain Reserves Group Ltd. (Sinograin), the largest grain storage and transportation corporation in China. Rampant corruption has been discovered within the corporation and its provincial and local branches. For instance, in 2015, Sinograin's storage managers in multiple provinces were found to have embezzled public funds by purchasing cheaper, low-quality grain for storage at high prices (*China Daily*, 2015). Corruption also takes place when state-owned agribusinesses seek domestic or overseas expansion. The Beidahuang Group is a case in point. The corporation was established based on the state farms created through reclamation campaigns in the 1950s and 1960s. Located in Heilongjiang province in northeast China, the corporation's state farms have been a major rice production base that could produce rice to meet the needs of 100 million people. Since the 2000s, the corporation ventured into risky M&As and expanded its business into manufacturing, the pharmaceutical industry, real estate, and finance. However, many of these ventures failed and several top managers were charged with corruption. These setbacks have had a negative effect on its rice production and food processing (*Sina*, 2016).

Regarding agricultural production within China, the assumption that large farms and agricultural companies will produce more grain and food stuffs than small farms is falsified. Research finds that large farms usually have higher labor productivity due to the economy of scale, but their production per unit of land is lower than that of small farms. This presents a problem for the Chinese state as its goal is to produce more grain and other agricultural products on the limited land within the country. A national survey in 2013 showed that large household farms produced less grain per unit of land than small ones (Tang et al., 2017). It also found that large family farms, which have been promoted as a new unit of operation and whose average size is about 12 hectares, also produce less grain per unit of land than small household farms (He, 2016; Du and Han, 2020). In addition, the Chinese state is concerned about the trend of more farmland being used for profitable cash crops than grain crops, a phenomenon called the "nongrain conversion of farmland" (耕地非粮化) in China, as this will reduce grain production and jeopardize the goal of grain security. Research finds that large farms are much more likely to use farmland for cash crops than small farms. A 2018 survey by the Chinese Academy of Social Sciences showed that farms below 13 hectares used most of their land for grain crops, but as farm size increased, the proportion of land used for grain crops decreased rapidly and the farms larger than 67 hectares only used 30 percent of the land for grain crops (Du and Han, 2020: 4–5). These problems have been noted by the Chinese state in recent years, prompting the central government to reiterate the caution against the "rash" or "forced" transfer of farmland to large farms (Han, 2019).

The key issue regarding grain farming by rural households is not their capability to produce more grain or adopt modern technology, as agricultural modernists have claimed, but their incentive to farm grain. Research finds that rural households tend to cultivate farmland less intensively if agricultural prices are low or if there are alternative wage employment activities (Gong and Zhang, 2017; Zhan and Huang, 2017). Urban-industrial development, the integration into the global food system, and the increasing dominance of agribusinesses have all contributed to low returns for small-scale farming as food imports have flooded the Chinese market. As a result, young people have left for the cities while some rural households only farm crops for self-consumption. This gives the Chinese governments, particularly local governments, another reason to promote land transfer to large farms. However, the expansion of large farms does not necessarily lead to an increase in grain production, and land concentrations would also create rural poverty and trigger peasant resistance. As a result, the Chinese state has issued contradictory policies to both protect farming households and support large farms (Hayward, 2017), which often puzzle the observers.

In summary, the interest to build global agribusinesses and the project of agricultural industrialization motivated the Chinese state to support the expansion of agrarian capital both domestically and overseas, giving rise to state-led agrarian capitalism. The Chinese state believes that this will contribute to food security. Representatives of agrarian capital, including large agribusiness corporations, dragonheads of various sizes, and large farms, have responded actively by emphasizing their control of the "whole supply chain" or the capability to produce grain and food stuffs. The analysis in this section shows, however, that such state-capital alliance does not lead to a more secure supply of food.

6 Resistance, Grassroots Movements, and Alternative Visions

The strategy to optimize the national–global food duality entails that China must maintain a high level of domestic grain production. As a major food importer, China is also interested in increasing the overall global supply of food so that the country could import more food from the global market. Such a productivist stance is highly in tune with the expansion strategy of corporate capital, which often emphasizes their role in supplying technology and investment to boost agricultural production (Fouilleux et al., 2017; McKeon, 2021). However, built on trade liberalization and capitalist agriculture, the strategy to optimize the national–global food duality would displace hundreds of millions of small producers in China from land. The push for a higher grain production has also placed enormous pressure on the environment. Furthermore, the pursuit of more food in the capitalist agri-food system turns food into a fictitious commodity, as defined by Karl Polanyi: Food is bought and sold according to the market logic while being stripped of its social-cultural significance (Polanyi, 2001 [1944]; McClintock, 2010). The food-for-profit drive has resulted in serious food safety issues in China, evidenced by many food safety scandals, with the widely known melamine-tainted milk incident in 2008 being just one example (Yan, 2012).

This section employs Karl Polanyi's framework to explicate the pernicious effects of China's global food strategy. The section focuses on the issues of land, labor, the environment, and food safety. The capitalist agri-food system in China has been confronted with countermovements at the grassroots level (Day, 2008), which have challenged and pushed back the capitalist logic of food production, distribution, and consumption, and offered alternative visions on food security. The section mainly investigates the contradictions of the agri-food system within China, but the findings are also relevant to the country's overseas engagement.

6.1 Dispossession, Precarization, and Land Struggles

The Chinese state implemented a nationwide land reform in the early 1950s and redistributed land from landlords to peasants. Only a few years later, the communist party-state launched the collectivization campaigns, which turned household farms into collective farms, organized in the forms of communes, brigades, and production teams (see Section 2.1). After 1978, rural reform replaced collective farms with the HRS, under which rural households *contract* use rights of land from the village, but the ownership of land belongs to the village collective (村集体). The two-right system, that is, the use right and the ownership right, had been in place until 2013. To facilitate land transfer from peasant households to new units of operation, the Chinese state changed the two-right system to a system of three rights in 2014: contract right, operation right (经营权), and ownership right. Peasant households hold the contract right, but they are urged to transfer the operation right to others, whereas the village collective still holds the ownership (Zhan, 2020a). The separation of the contract right and the operation right suggests that peasant households need not necessarily farm the land that they contracted.

Presently, the Chinese state encourages the transfer of the operation right to large farms, but it affirms the commitment to protecting the contract right of peasant households. In November 2019, the central government stipulated that peasant households could extend the land contract for another thirty years until the 2050s. Thus, a main form of farmland dispossession in the Chinese context is that peasant households are forced to transfer out the operation right. It is partial dispossession as peasant households will receive rent from the party that takes the operation right, be it another household, a rural cooperative, a large family farm, or an agricultural company. It can also be seen as the commodification of the operation right of farmland, albeit with varying degrees of coercion depending on local government policy. The Chinese case highlights the complexity and diverse patterns of agrarian transition and dispossession at national and subnational levels (Bair et al., 2019).

After transferring out the operation right, most peasants will have to seek wage employment in the city. Over the last decade, the Chinese governments at central and local levels have been pushing to accelerate urbanization and move more people to the city (Zhan, 2017b). In 2020, the urbanization rate, that is, the share of urban population, reached 64 percent, having increased from 50 percent in 2010. In other words, within just ten years, China, with a population of 1.4 billion, had moved nearly 200 million people from the countryside to the city. However, the data on urban population include rural migrants in the city. If only people who hold urban *hukou* (i.e., urban household registration) were counted, the urbanization rate was only 45.5 percent in 2020. That is, 261 million, or 18.5 percent of the population, were registered as rural residents but working and living in the city (National Bureau of Statistics [NBS], 2021b). Why is there such a large urban population registered as rural residents under China's household registration system? Put another way, why did they not change their registration to urban *hukou*? Large national surveys and my own research have found that rural populations who migrate to the city are unwilling to change their *hukou* status. This is primarily because they want to keep rural land rights, which are conditioned on rural *hukou* status (Zhang, 2011; Andreas and Zhan, 2016).

Although rural migrants work in the city, the jobs that they find are often low-wage ones without employment security. Due to labor reforms and informalization since the 1990s, the Chinese urban labor market has witnessed an increasing degree of precarity (Lee, 2016, 2019). Positioned in lower social strata of the urban society, most rural migrants must bear low-wage, insecure, and contract jobs in sectors such as construction, retail services, assembly-line manufacturing, and more recently, the platform economy (Chan, 2021). The heightened urban precarity suggests that rural migrants are at a high risk of losing jobs, particularly during economic downturns or crises. For example, urban employers laid off 25 million migrant workers during the 2008 financial crisis, who were forced to return to rural areas (Wen, 2012: 211–212). Migrant workers also bore the brunt of the COVID-19 pandemic, and national statistics show that the number of rural migrant workers decreased by 2.7 percent in 2020. This suggests that about 4.7 million migrants lost their jobs in the city. However, the statistics did not count tens of millions of rural migrants who were unable to find work in the early months of the outbreak, that is, from February to May 2020 (Zhan, 2020b; National Bureau of Statistics [NBS], 2021c).

The struggles over further commodification of land and labor have been the main manifestations of the Polanyian double movement in China (also see Chuang, 2020). The concern over food security prompted the Chinese state to support land transfer to large farms, which accelerates the transition to agrarian capitalism and the proletarianization of rural labor. However, peasants and rural migrants hold onto their land rights by not changing *hukou* status and thus resist the full commodification of land and the full proletarianization of labor (Zhan and Scully, 2018). This has given rise to struggles over land between local government, agrarian capital, and peasants. Local governments pursue urbanization by moving rural residents to the city, and they support land transfer to large farms. In recent years, local governments attempted to coerce more rural migrants to register for urban *hukou*. Agribusinesses and large farms are not satisfied with the partial control of land as they must pay rent to peasants, who hold the contract right. This decreases the profitability of agriculture and grain production. In recent years, there have been increasing voices from agribusiness companies and large farms on how grain farming is not profitable. They either push local governments to provide more subsidies or argue that they should take full control of land (Du and Han, 2020; Wu and Liu, 2020).

6.2 Spatial Fix, Environmental Degradation, and Food Safety

The need to maintain a high level of domestic grain production has placed enormous pressure on the environment. The problem and its manifestations, however, vary from place to place within China. With the deepening of the capitalist transition of the Chinese economy since the 1990s, the contradiction between economic growth and grain production has intensified. This is because agriculture, particularly grain production, is much less profitable than urban and industrial activities. Thus, local governments and private actors tend to allocate resources such as land and water to urban and industrial sectors rather than grain farming. Since the 1990s, rapid urbanization and industrialization have turned coastal provinces such as Guangdong, Zhejiang, Jiangsu, and Fujian into the "world factory." The lands there that were previously used for agriculture were converted to industrial and urban lands. Between 1990 and 2010, the area of urban and industrial lands doubled from 25,600 to 49,700 square kilometers in coastal provinces, up by 24,100 square kilometers. That is, nearly 2.4 million hectares of farmland and other lands were converted to nonagricultural usages (Kuang et al., 2016). The coastal provinces were previously the main sites for grain crops in China, but grain production has declined there in the last two decades due to urbanization and industrialization. Between 1996 and 2014, grain production in Zhejiang, Guangdong, and Fujian provinces decreased from 15.2 to 7.6 million tonnes, 18.4 to 13.6 million tonnes, and 9.5 to 3.7 million tonnes, respectively, and the decline also occurred in coastal areas of Jiangsu province (Zhan and Huang, 2017: 142). Meanwhile, grain production in northern and inland provinces increased, this not only made up the loss in coastal provinces but also led to growth in grain production since 2004. This can be regarded as a process of spatial fix, that is, the problem of declining grain production is fixed by moving the main sites of grain production from economically developed regions to less developed regions within China (Harvey, 1981; Zhan and Huang, 2017). The spatial fix in grain production has been driven by the dynamics of capitalist accumulation and state policy. The acceleration of capitalist accumulation in coastal regions has reduced land areas for grain production, whereas inland and northern regions have increased grain production because the tension between profitability and grain production there is less intense and because these regions' agricultural land is relatively larger. Furthermore, the Chinese state has provided large amounts of subsidies and development funds to support grain production in northern and inland provinces (Zhan and Huang, 2017).

The spatial fix enables China to maintain and even increase grain production, but this has created pressure on the environment, as the fix increased grain production in regions where soil and climate are unsuitable for intensive farming. Although farmland areas in northern provinces are relatively large, all but three northeast provinces have faced the problem of water shortage due to low levels of precipitation. The expansion of grain production in the North China Plain, the northwest, and Inner Mongolia has led to overdrafting of the groundwater, exacerbating the problems of groundwater depletion and desert-ification (Kong et al., 2016). The intensification of grain farming has also contributed to soil degradation, and this has become a problem even for the northeast, which is known for its fertile farmland. It is found that the fertile black soil layer in the northeast has been thinning rapidly, to the extent that intensive farming would be unsustainable in the future (Gong et al., 2013).

The spatial fix has exacerbated soil and water pollution. The application of high levels of chemical fertilizers and pesticides in order to increase production has severely polluted water and soil, which in turn affects the quality of grain and other agricultural products (Zou et al., 2020). In the last two decades, intensive animal production has emerged as another source of agricultural pollution as large-scale, industrial livestock production replaced household animal husbandry (Hu et al., 2017a). Industrial factories have also negatively affected grain production. Although the spatial fix has to some extent shifted some grain production away from industrialized coastal and southern provinces, it is still necessary for these provinces to maintain significant levels of grain production for national grain security. As a result, industrial zones are often located adjacent to areas of agricultural production, and the wastes and pollu-tants discharged from industrial facilities have affected water and soil for grain crops. It is estimated that a fifth of agricultural land in China is polluted, to varying degrees, by heavy metals. For example, it was reported that rice from some areas of South China was contaminated with harmful cadmium (*Nanfang Daily*, 2013: 6).

The worsening environmental degradation has threatened the sustainability of domestic food production and food safety in China, which in turn would undermine the efforts to maintain an optimal national–global food duality. The environmental problems have become a serious concern of the Chinese state. In the last two decades, the government has taken multiple measures to protect the environment for agriculture and grain production. These measures include, but are not limited to: i. stabilizing and decreasing the use of chemical fertilizers and pesticides; ii. protecting the black soil layer in the northeast; iii. applying water-saving technologies; iv. reducing the sown area for corn while increasing that for soybeans; and v. remediating heavy-metal polluted soil in South China. However, to what extent these measures will be effective remains unanswered. The previous analysis shows that the transition to capitalist agriculture and the dependence on large and corporate farms, which have given rise to an industrial agriculture in China, will likely perpetuate the problem of environmental degradation, if not worsen it (Kimbrell, 2002; Woodhouse, 2010).

Due to heavy uses of agrochemical inputs, industrial agriculture also creates food safety problems that undermine human health, particularly in the context of weak regulations (McKay and Veltmeyer, 2021). In China, this has manifested in numerous food safety incidents and scandals in the last two decades (Wu and Chen, 2013). Widespread food safety problems have eroded people's trust in political and market institutions (Yan, 2012; Wu et al., 2017). According to a national survey in 2010, 68 percent of the respondents lacked a sense of food safety, while 95 percent held that the food system in China was problematic. The survey also showed that the respondents were most concerned about the following food safety problems: meat of sick animals; pesticide/herbicide residues in vegetables and fruits; illegal additives; toxic foods; gutter oil; high levels of hormones; high levels of heavy metals; and veterinary drug residues in meat. The respondents attributed the food safety problems to immoral profit-seeking activities and weak regulations (Ouyang, 2011). The food safety crisis has given rise to grassroots movements and practices in China that attempt to produce and obtain food products beyond the profit-oriented capitalist agri-food system, and these movements have coalesced with those that explore alternative agricultural and rural development models.

6.3 Grassroots Movements and Alternative Visions

The countermovements at the grassroots level in China can be classified into two categories: organized and unorganized movements. This section is focused on organized movements, but unorganized movements, particularly resistance and struggles waged by peasants, are no less important than organized ones in terms of social and policy impacts. Unorganized movements refer to spontaneous resistance by peasants and villages when they face land dispossession or other injustices. The most important unorganized movement in China is arguably peasants' resistance to full land dispossession in the process of urbanization and industrialization, which has led to tens of thousands of protests and sometimes violent clashes between peasants and local authorities each year. Since the 1990s, local governments in China enclosed and expropriated large tracts of peasants' farmlands and homesteads for urban and industrial projects such as real estate, factories, and infrastructure works, and often provided insufficient compensation for peasants' land loss. Peasants resisted land expropriation and fought for higher levels of compensation (Sargeson, 2013; Andreas et al., 2020). Some villages were able to collectively fight for land rights. For instance, the collective resistance of Wukan Village in Guangdong province against land grabs between 2011 and 2016 has drawn wide attention and is regarded as an exemplar case of grassroots resistance in China (Hess, 2015). Although the unorganized movements including land struggles have been unable to halt land dispossession and other injustices in China, they exerted great pressure on the Chinese state and forced it to accommodate some of the peasants' demands (Lee and Zhang, 2013; Zhan, 2019b). Furthermore, the unorganized movements have also drawn the attention of the public and even some government officials to the views of organized movements.

Organized grassroots movements offer alternative views to the seemingly inevitable transition to a capitalist agri-food system in China. They also challenge the productivist doctrine in the Chinese state's global food strategy by highlighting the importance of smallholder-based rural development, sustainability, food quality, and social and ecological dimensions of food production and consumption. These movements are influenced by the historical legacy of rural activism and socialism in China as well as by global movements against agrarian capitalism and corporate power. This section introduces three major grassroots movements in China: the Rural Reconstruction Movement (RRM), alternative food networks (AFNs), and the food sovereignty movement. It should be noted that participants in these movements are sometimes the same people and that the movements are not contradictory but complementary.

6.3.1 Rural Reconstruction Movement

The most influential rural grassroots movement in China is arguably the RRM (乡村建设运动), which has not only made a significant social impact but also influenced the country's rural policy. The movement claims the legacy from the rural construction movement in the 1930s, thus it is also known as the New Rural Reconstruction Movement (NRRM). In the 1930s, Chinese scholars such as Liang Shumin and James Yen experimented with reconstructing rural China as a third way to save the nation, which was distinguished from Western capitalism and communism. Liang and Yen established rural schools and mobilized peasants to join rural cooperatives (Yan and Chen, 2013). The contemporary RRM also aims to find an alternative way to develop the Chinese countryside. In the mid-1990s, the key founder of the movement, Wen Tiejun, who was previously a researcher working for government-funded research institutes and later a professor at Renmin University, coined the term of "Three Rural Problems" (三农问题) to capture the rural crisis at the time. Wen and other participants of RRM contend that modernization and capitalist agriculture, proposed by some liberal economists and supported by the Chinese state, are the cause of rather than the solution to the rural crisis. The movement started in the early 2000s, and it attracted university professors and students, intellectuals, representatives of NGOs, and grassroots activists. The movement organized national conferences, established RRM-themed NGOs, and mobilized peasants to join rural cooperatives and mutual-aid groups. As the movement spread over the past two decades, there have emerged different experiments within the movement. Some experiments established comprehensive rural cooperatives based on the experiences of Japan, South Korea, and Taiwan; some focused on the rural credit cooperatives or other specialized rural cooperatives; some made efforts to create or strengthen rural grassroots organizations, including official organizations such as the party branch and the village committee; and some endeavored to organize villagers to participate in cultural and educational activities (Yan and Chen, 2013; Si and Scott, 2016; Yang et al., 2018). A common feature of these experiments is that they promote autonomous rural development by and for rural communities and villagers while opposing the growing power of agribusiness companies and private large farms in rural areas.

The movement occurred at a time when the Chines state was also looking for ideas to mitigate the rural crisis. In 2004, the central government initiated the strategy of "building a new socialist countryside," and laid out a series of prorural policies and measures, some of which were proposed by the RRM (Ahlers, 2014). In the meantime, the key figures in the movement were invited by the central government for policy consultation and the activities of the movement were also reported in state media. Thus, it was commonly believed that the movement had some influence on the central government's prorural policy initiatives. In 2006, the central government enacted a law to support specialized farmers cooperatives, which was a key proposal of the movement. In 2017, the Xi Jinping administration launched the strategy of rural revitalization (乡村振兴) to promote rural development and improve rural livelihoods; this initiative might also have been influenced by the movement.

However, the policy initiatives of the Chinese state are often at odds with the movement's aims. For example, despite the movement's opposition to the dominance of large agrarian capital in agriculture, the Chinse state has been consistently promoting and supporting the expansion of agribusiness companies and large farms over the past two decades. The movement has also not at all changed the Chinese state's position on modernization and urbanization. Furthermore, although the number of rural cooperatives, advocated by the RRM, had greatly increased to more than 2 million due to government support, research finds that more than 90 percent of the cooperatives are not genuine cooperatives as they were set up or are controlled by powerful agricultural households, large farms, and agribusiness companies (Hu et al., 2017b; Day and Schneider, 2018). The Chinese state has no intention of regulating these cooperatives as they serve to transfer land from peasant households. Nevertheless, the prorural policies and rhetoric of the state have created political space for the participants of the movement to continue their experiments in rural areas.

6.3.2 Alternative Food Networks

The RRM is not specifically focused on the food system but aims to promote rural development including agriculture. The food safety crisis that emerged in the 2000s motivated some participants of the RRM to establish AFNs (Si and Scott, 2016). Influenced by the AFN movement in Western countries, the practitioners of AFNs in China aim to supply organic and safe foods to urban consumers who are anxious about the safety of foods sold in supermarkets (Scott et al., 2018). The participants of the movement have made efforts to connect urban consumers with small farmers who produce vegetables, fruits, meat, and grain in ecological ways, most importantly, using fewer or no agrochemicals. The movement aims to remove the intermediaries such as agribusiness companies and supermarkets between food producers and consumers, and this will enable small farmers to sell their products at higher prices while urban consumers can purchase safe foods directly from producers. The most common AFNs in China comprise Community-Supported Agriculture (CSA), farmers' markets, buying clubs, and in recent years, Taobao stores and WeChat shops.

The experiments of CSA farms in China started around the mid-2000s. Adapted from practices in the United States and Canada, the CSA practitioners invited urban consumers to subscribe to CSA farms. The subscribers pay the farms in advance for seasonal harvests, and the farms deliver a box of in-season vegetables, fruits, and other farm products weekly or biweekly to the subscriber. Urban subscribers are also invited for on-site visits so that they could interact with farmers and inspect farming practices in these farms (Si et al., 2015). A variant of CSA in China is that some scholar activists use the CSA model to alleviate rural poverty by promoting food products of a particular village or several villages. For instance, a research team from the China Agricultural University established a "nested market" between Beijing consumers and a poor village in Hebei province, which is about 200 kilometers from the national capital. The research team, together with the village committee, organized dozens of poor households in the village to supply a wide array of organic or safe food products to hundreds of consumers in Beijing. The ongoing experiment was started in 2010, and both participant rural households and Beijing consumers have been increasing in number. The researchers argue that the nested market has successfully bypassed the intermediaries in the hourglass structure in the corporate-dominated food system, improved the livelihoods of poor households, and met the demand of urban consumers for safe, trustable food products (van der Ploeg et al., 2012; Ye and He, 2020).

Farmers' markets and buying clubs are also alternative venues for urban consumers to purchase safe and quality foods. Farmers' markets have been held regularly in several large cities in the last decade and these markets invite approved organic farms to participate. Buying clubs are mainly initiated by middle-class urban consumers who source safe and quality food directly from rural producers. Different from the CSA model, urban consumers participating in farmers' markets and buying clubs are less concerned about whether foods are made by small farmers or poor households, and their primary concern is whether foods are produced in organic and safe ways (Si et al., 2015). Nevertheless, many small farmers and rural households who produce organic foods have benefited from such AFNs. The expansion of farmers' markets and buying clubs has been facilitated by social media platforms such as WeChat, which have made it much easier to spread information of farmers' markets and recruit new club members. The payment function of WeChat and other e-payment methods have also made it very convenient to make transactions between farmers and consumers.

The wide use of social media and e-commerce platforms also gave rise to a great number of Taobao (the largest e-commerce platform in China) stores and WeChat shops that sell food products directly from farms to urban consumers (Qi et al., 2019; Martindale, 2021). The convenience of marketing food products through these platforms has attracted some educated rural youths to return to the countryside for organic farming who would otherwise stay in the city as rural migrants. The food safety crisis has also raised the awareness of food safety among peasants, who started to realize the value of organic foods. Research finds that a growing number of peasant households produce organic foods either for self-consumption or as gifts for relatives and friends in the city (Si et al., 2019).

Various AFNs provide an alternative to the capitalist agri-food system, but there are contradictions within the movement (Si et al., 2015; Day and Schneider, 2018). First, organic foods marketed through AFNs such as CSA, farmers' markets, buying clubs, and online stores are often priced several times higher than regular products in supermarkets. Thus, only a small proportion of affluent urban consumers can afford them. Second, small farms and peasant households that supply these products are also subjected to market rules.

To reduce costs and increase production, some of them often apply chemical fertilizers and pesticides, albeit at low levels. As a result, it is difficult to distinguish between foods that are strictly produced in organic ways and those produced with some use of agrochemicals. This sometimes creates distrust between small farmers and urban consumers. Third, agribusiness companies, large farms, and supermarkets have seen the growing market of organic foods as a profit-making opportunity. Their participation in the production and distribution of organic foods increased competition and is reducing the space for AFNs. It is found that some CSA farms and farmers' markets must operate like agribusiness companies to make profits (Day and Schneider, 2018). Nevertheless, various AFNs provide alternative ways of food production and distribution, and their expansion has offered opportunities for small farmers and small traders.

6.3.3 Food Sovereignty Movement

The food sovereignty movement in China is a nascent movement that grew out of the influence of the transnational peasants' movement La Via Campesina (LVC) and the domestic RRM and AFNs noted earlier. La Via Campesina introduced the concept of food sovereignty in the World Food Summit in 1996, which was defined as follows: "Food sovereignty is the right of peoples to healthy and culturally appropriate food produced through ecologically sound and sustainable methods, and their right to define their own food and agriculture systems. It puts those who produce, distribute and consume food at the heart of food systems and policies rather than the demands of markets and corporations" (La Via Campesina [LVC], 2007).

A key representative of the food sovereignty movement in China is the people's Food Sovereignty Network in China (FSNC), which was formed in 2013 (Gaudreau, 2019; Yan et al., 2021). The FSNC has grown out of the RRM and AFNs in China, and it represents a food sovereignty movement with Chinese characteristics. The FSNC's advocacy contributes to the global food sovereignty movement in two important ways. First, the network is sympathetic to the efforts to protect peasants' land rights and promote a smallholder rural economy, but it argues that it might be a futile effort to build a peasant economy as individual peasant households and small farmers are too weak to fight the power of agribusiness companies and corporate farms. Thus, in the Chinese context, it proposes strengthening the power of the village collective, which should not only hold the nominal land ownership but also the operation right. In so doing, the village could allocate village resources together and fend off the incursion of large agrarian capital. Second, the FSNC proposes a vision of ecological collectivism to address the ecological crisis caused by the capitalist agri-food system (Yan et al., 2021). The network highlights the importance of rural cooperatives, indigenous agricultural knowledge, and China's socialist legacy of solidarity building among peasants. The goal is to build a collective effort to resist the penetration of industrial agriculture and creatively apply indigenous knowledge and technology to reduce the use of agrochemicals and other harmful inputs.

Since its inception, the FSNC has carried out its advocacy through its website, WeChat, and other social media outlets, organized annual conferences, disseminated the publications of its group field research findings, and held online talk series and study sessions. The network has also made efforts to build connections with several villages that agree with its visions.

In summary, the expansion of the capitalist agri-food system in China under the aegis of the country's global food strategy has met with the countermovements at the grassroots level. These movements have challenged the modernist discourse and the productivist doctrine while opening up the space for debating the possibility of building alternative systems in China. How effective these movements will be in challenging agrarian capitalism and corporate power remains unanswered. Nevertheless, so far, these movements have to some extent resisted a full-scale onslaught of agribusiness corporations and private large farms in China, evidenced by the partial dispossession of peasants' land rights and the Chinese state' continuing emphasis (at least rhetorically) on the importance of peasant households and village communities in the ongoing campaign of rural revitalization.

7 Conclusion: Agri-Food Reordering in the Twenty-first Century

In less than half a century (1978–2020), China has transformed itself from a country that barely fed itself to a powerful player in the global food system, characterized by massive food imports, active overseas agricultural engagement, and the global expansion of Chinese agribusiness. While the rising food demand of China aroused anxiety over global food security, this Element has made efforts to move beyond the literature on "who will feed China" and examined various dimensions of the country's global food strategy. Based on analysis of China's overseas food engagement and its domestic dynamics, this Element argues that the country's strategy can be best described as pursuing an optimal national–global food duality, which is premised on actively utilizing overseas agri-food resources whist maintaining a high level of domestic food production.

This global food strategy distinguishes China from other major food powers and previous hegemons in the capitalist world economy. First, as a food importer, China is apparently different from the United States, which was the hegemon in the postwar global food regime (Friedmann and McMichael, 1989). While the United States as a food exporter actively sought to penetrate the food market of other countries, China is interested in creasing the global supply of food, particularly from the Global South, so that it can diversify food import sources. Second, China's food strategy is distinct from that of the British Empire in the nineteenth century, despite both being food importers. The British Empire was able to outsource food and agricultural resources through colonialism and overseas agricultural settlements, but China must face a volatile global food market and the uncertainties in importing agri-food commodities. An integral component of the country's food strategy is to maintain a high level of domestic production so that it can withhold, at least temporarily, the disruption of overseas food supply. This also gives the country some leeway for adjusting levels and categories of food imports when bargaining with food exporters. Third, China must depend on the global market for food, but the country is different from its East Asian neighbors in terms of the degree of import dependence. With a population of 1.4 billion, China will unlikely lower the food self-sufficiency ratio, that is, the ratio of domestic production in total food consumption, to the levels of Japan, South Korea, and Taiwan. Otherwise, the country would have to quadruple its already enormous food imports and face an extremely vulnerable food security situation.

The growing influence of China in the global food system will profoundly alter the international agri-food order in the twenty-first century. It will further erode the dominance of northern countries whilst increasing the share of the Global South in the export market. In addition, the interdependence of China and NACs, such as Brazil, Argentina, Russia, South Africa, Thailand, Vietnam, and Indonesia, will form a powerful bloc or blocs in the system of global food governance, which may revise or challenge existing rules and norms on agri-food production, distribution, and consumption. The impact of China's global food strategy will be uneven across regions and manifest differently in various countries. Based on the analysis in the preceding sections, this Element makes the following preliminary projections. China's impact will be strongly felt in the exporting countries that are geographically close to China. In Southeast Asia, Myanmar, Laos, and Cambodia will see food exports to China continuing to grow, and agricultural investment from China will also push the frontiers of crop production there to expand. These three countries and Vietnam will become major sources of cereal imports (rice in particular) for China, substituting traditional exporters such as Thailand and the United States. China's demand will also increase food exports of Russia, Central Asia, and Eastern Europe, deepening their food export dependence. China will increasingly source resource-intensive foods from countries in EU and Oceania, particularly meat, milk, seafood, and wine, registering higher food trade deficiencies with these countries. However, the food relations between China and these countries will be subject to the ongoing US–China rivalry, thus frequent fluctuations and disruptions in food trade and agricultural investment are anticipated. In Africa, China will not seek to import large volumes of cereals there but will likely stimulate, through agricultural aids or investments, the production and export of commercial crops, such as oil crops, fruits, nuts, and coffee. China and South American countries will maintain and even strengthen the soybean–livestock complex to meet the growing demand for meat and oils in China, and China is also interested to import meat, seafood, sugar, and fruits directly from the continent. Due to the US–China rivalry, the food trade between China and North America will be unstable, but in the short term, the strong agri-food trade relations between China and North America will persist, as neither side could find enough alternative sources of imports or exports.

Although China will reshape the international agri-food order in profound ways, this Element does not suggest that a China-centered food regime will emerge, at least in the short term (the coming decade or so). First, the US–China rivalry and the trend of growing protectionism make it extremely unlikely that all nations will forge a consensus on how to govern the global food system. The instabilities and tensions in global food governance described by Pritchard (2009) will persist, if not worsen (also see Hopewell, 2020). Furthermore, China appears not to be interested in taking the lead in making new rules for global food governance. This is evidenced by the country's low-profile presence in the recent UN Food Systems Summit. Second, the support of the Chinese state for corporate capital both within and beyond its borders makes China an unlikely candidate for challenging the dominance of corporate power in the global food system. It is also difficult for the Chinese state to rein in its agribusiness corporations to give up short-term profits for long-term food security when the two diverge in the future, as shown in Section 5. Third, the strategy of optimizing the national–global food duality places more emphasis on securing national food supply, both through domestic production and by sourcing food from overseas, than on global food governance. It has not offered a clear alternative vision of global food governance for other countries, NGOs, and grass-roots movements to follow.

China's global food strategy will affect global food security both negatively and positively. On the negative side, the productivist orientation of China's food strategy will boost food supply worldwide and draw more low-income countries into export agriculture, this will deepen the export dependency of low-income countries and subject them to the volatility of the global market. Furthermore, the expansion of production will add growing stress on an already vulnerable environment and accelerate the pace of climate change, which will exacerbate global food insecurity in the long term. Second, China's support for the corporate governance of the global food system will place small farmers and consumers at a disadvantage. Under corporate governance, small farmers in developing countries are subject to the dominant power of large agribusiness companies, in agricultural production as well as in the markets for inputs and food products. This engenders farmer indebtedness, food insecurity, and malnutrition of the low-income groups. Third, China's rising demand will intensify global competition for food. Although this will not significantly affect low-income countries' access to staple foods in the global market as China largely maintains self-sufficiency on cereals (Section 3), it may affect middle-income countries' dietary transition as the competition for food increases the prices of protein-rich foods, such as meat, milk, and aquatic products.

China's global food strategy may also have positive effects on global food security. The country's high demand for food and efforts to diversify imports will lead more countries, particularly southern countries, to increase food exports. This would increase small farmers' income in the export sectors and hence their access to food. However, this depends on whether small farmers in the exporting countries have secure land rights and can benefit from growing exports. In addition, as a top food importer, China will play a role different from food exporters such as the United States and EU. To increase the global supply of food, China may provide agricultural aids and allow technological transfer to low-income countries in Africa and Asia, which presents an opportunity for these countries to develop agriculture and increase food security. China's emphasis on national food sovereignty, to some extent, lessens the constraints of the global food system on developing countries. In international negotiations, China supports the proposal that agricultural production must meet the domestic food needs before the agricultural products are exported or used for the production of biofuels. However, it remains unclear how China will act in future when facing the contradiction between its needs for food imports and the support for national food sovereignty of developing countries.

The Chinese state's strategy of allying with agrarian capital for food security will be diluted by the latter's short-term pursuit of profits, contributing to speculation and price fluctuations in the food market. The influx of food imports and the expansion of domestic and foreign agrarian capital also inevitably disrupt the household mode of food production in China, leading to exploitation and dispossession in the countryside and underemployment and precarity in the city, which in turn exacerbates food insecurity of low-income populations.

Thus, the pursuit of an optimal national–global food duality for food security is probably an illusion in that the strategy contains the contradictions that will undermine itself in the future. There have already been signs that the strategy is not working as intended. Externally, the attempts to support Chinese agribusiness to control the whole supply chain have not significantly mitigated the risks of overseas food supply, evidenced by frequent disruptions and restrictions as well as price hikes and fluctuations in recent years, both before and after the COVID-19 outbreak. Internally, the Chinese state has to pour a huge and yet growing sum in order to support agribusiness companies and large farms for grain production, but the latter often divert these funds for profitable nongrain crops or for other purposes. In the meantime, peasants and small farmers, previously the main force in grain production, are being squeezed out of agriculture. Many of them have turned into the urban poor who are unable to adequately feed themselves due to high food prices. The problems with China's food strategy make it necessary to look for alternative visions to build a sustainable and equitable food system, for which the emerging grassroots movements on rural development, food safety, and food sovereignty in China have much to offer.

References

Ahlers, A. (2014). *Rural Policy Implementation in Contemporary China: New Socialist Countryside*. Abingdon: Routledge.

Aksoy, M. A. (2004). The Evolution of Agricultural Trade Flows. In M. A. Aksoy & J. C. Beghin (eds.), *Global Agricultural Trade and Developing Countries* (pp. 17–35). Washington, DC: World Bank Publications.

Andreas, J., Kale, S. S., Levien, M., & Zhang, Q. F. (2020). Rural Land Dispossession in China and India. *Journal of Peasant Studies*, 47(6), 1109–1142.

Andreas, J., & Zhan, S. (2016). Hukou and Land: Market Reform and Rural Displacement in China. *Journal of Peasant Studies*, 43(4), 798–827.

Andrews, E. L. (2003). U.S. Moves to Limit Textile Imports from China. *New York Times*. November 19.

Arrighi, G., & Silver, B. (1999). *Chaos and Governance in the Modern World System*. Minneapolis: University of Minnesota Press.

Bailey, R., & Wellesley, L. (2017). *Chokepoints and Vulnerabilities in Global Food Trade*. London: Chatham House.

Bair, J., Harris, K., & Hough, P. A. (2019). Roads from Calabria: The Arrighian Approach to Agrarian Political Economy. *Journal of Agrarian Change*, 19(3), 391–406.

Beijing News. (2019). Imports of Russian Soybeans Are Permitted (允许从俄罗斯全境进口大豆). *Beijing News*. August 5. www.bjnews.com.cn/detail/156497218514190.html.

Belesky, P., & Lawrence, G. (2019). Chinese State Capitalism and Neomercantilism in the Contemporary Food Regime: Contradictions, Continuity and Change. *Journal of Peasant Studies*, 46(6), 1119–1141.

Bello, W. F. (2009). *The Food Wars*. London: Verso

Bernstein, H. (2016). Agrarian Political Economy and Modern World Capitalism: The Contributions of Food Regime Analysis. *Journal of Peasant Studies*, 43(3), 611–647.

Bernstein, T. P., & Lü, X. (2003). *Taxation without Representation in Contemporary Rural China*. Cambridge: Cambridge University Press.

Bhala, R. (1999). Enter the Dragon: An Essay on China's WTO Accession Saga. *American University International Law Review*, 15, 1469–1538.

Bitabarova, A. G. (2018). Unpacking Sino-Central Asian Engagement along the New Silk Road: A Case Study of Kazakhstan. *Journal of Contemporary East Asia Studies*, 7(2), 149–173.

Böhme, M. (2021). Shared Interest or Strategic Threat? A Critical Investigation of Political Debates and Regulatory Responses to Chinese Agricultural Investment in Australia. *Globalizations*, 18(3), 441–460.

Borras Jr., S. M., Hall, R., Scoones, I., White, B., & Wolford, W. (2011). Towards a Better Understanding of Global Land Grabbing: An Editorial Introduction. *Journal of Peasant Studies*, 38(2), 209–216.

Bosley, C. (2019). Chinese Ambassador Says ChemChina's Syngenta Purchase Was a Mistake. *Bloomberg*. June 29. www.bloomberg.com/news/articles/2019-06-29/chinese-ambassador-says-chemchina-s-syngenta-purchase-a-mistake.

Bramall, C. (2004). Chinese Land Reform in Long-Run Perspective and in the Wider East Asian Context. *Journal of Agrarian Change*, 4(1–2), 107–141.

Bramall, C. (2009). *Chinese Economic Development*. Abingdon: Routledge.

Bratspies, R. (2017). Owning All the Seeds: Consolidation and Control in Agbiotech. *Environmental Law*, 47, 583–608.

Bräutigam, D. (2015). *Will Africa Feed China?* Oxford: Oxford University Press.

Bräutigam, D., & Ekman, S.-M. S. (2012). Briefing Rumours and Realities of Chinese Agricultural Engagement in Mozambique. *African Affairs*, 111(444), 483–492.

Brown, L. R. (1994). Who Will Feed China? *World Watch*, 7(5), 10–19.

Brown, L. R. (1995). *Who Will Feed China? Wake-Up Call for a Small Planet*. New York: WW Norton & Company.

Brown, L. R. (2011). Can the United States Feed China? *Washington Post*. March 13.

Brown, L. R. (2014). *Can the World Feed China?* Washington, DC: Earth Policy Institute.

CCTV. (2020). The World Is on the Verge of a Serious Food Crisis, Will It Affect Chinese People's Rice Bag? (世界濒临严重粮食危机, 中国老百姓的 "米袋子" 会受影响吗). August 4. http://news.cctv.com/2020/08/04/ARTItLjAsrpA5skxCyyA1isY200804.shtml.

Chai, Y., Pardey, P. G., Chan-Kang, C. et al. (2019). Passing the Food and Agricultural R&D Buck? The United States and China. *Food Policy*, 86, 101729.

Chakrabortty, A. (2008). Secret Report: Biofuel Caused Food Crisis. *Guardian*. July 3.

Chan, J. (2021). Hunger for Profit: How Food Delivery Platforms Manage Couriers in China. *Sociologias*, 23, 58–82.

Chang, A.-L. (2019). Singapore Sets 30% Goal for Home-Grown Food by 2030. *The Straits Times*. March 8.

Chen, X. (2012). Food Trade More Effective than Farming Overseas (海外种地不如贸易). *China Entrepreneur*, 28(11), 26.

Chen, Y., Li, X., Wang, L., & Wang, S. (2017). Is China Different from Other Investors in Global Land Acquisition? Some Observations from Existing Deals in China's Going Global Strategy. *Land Use Policy*, 60, 362–372.

Chheang, V. (2017). *The Political Economy of Chinese Investment in Cambodia*. Singapore: ISEAS Publishing.

China Daily. (2015). Corruption in Grain Storage SOE Should Never Be Ignored. *China Daily*. April 20. www.chinadaily.com.cn/opinion/2015-04/20/content_20478525.htm.

China National Cereals, Oils and Foodstuffs Corporation (COFCO). (2021). History and Honor. www.cofco.com/en/AboutCOFCO/HistoryandHonor/.

China National Development and Reform Commission (NDRC) (2008). Instructions on Promoting the Healthy Development of the Soybean Industry (促进大豆加工业健康发展的指导意见). www.gov.cn/zwgk/2008-09/03/content_1086321.htm.

China National Development and Reform Commission (NDRC). (2015). *Vision and Actions on Jointly Building Silk Road Economic Belt and 21st Century Maritime Silk Road*. Beijing: People's Publishing House.

Christiansen, F. (2009). Food Security, Urbanization and Social Stability in China. *Journal of Agrarian Change*, 9(4), 548–575.

Chuang, J. (2020). *Beneath the China Boom: Labor, Citizenship, and the Making of a Rural Land Market*. Oakland: University of California Press.

Clapp, J. (2006). WTO Agriculture Negotiations: Implications for the Global South. *Third World Quarterly*, 27(4), 563–577.

Clapp, J. (2014). Financialization, Distance and Global Food Politics. *Journal of Peasant Studies*, 41(5), 797–814.

Clapp, J. (2017). Food Self-Sufficiency: Making Sense of It, and When It Makes Sense. *Food Policy*, 66, 88–96.

Dai, M., & Zhang, X. (2012). Regulatory Talks Difficult to Prevent COFCO's Price Hikes: Is Its Control of the Market for Food Security or for Profit? (约谈难抑中粮涨价冲动 掌握市场话语权为安全?为利润?). *Workers' Daily*. August 1.

Day, A. (2008). The End of the Peasant? New Rural Reconstruction in China. *Boundary 2*, 35(2), 49–73.

Day, A. F., & Schneider, M. (2018). The End of Alternatives? Capitalist Transformation, Rural Activism and the Politics of Possibility in China. *Journal of Peasant Studies*, 45(7), 1221–1246.

Du, Z., & Han, L. (2020). The Impact of Production-Side Changes in Grain Supply on China's Food Security (供给侧生产端变化对中国粮食安全的影响研究). *Chinese Rural Economy* 36(4), 2–14.

Duggan, N., & Naarajärvi, T. (2015). China in Global Food Security Governance. *Journal of Contemporary China*, 24(95), 943–960.

Edelman, M., Weis, T., Baviskar, A. et al. (2014). Introduction: Critical Perspectives on Food Sovereignty. *Journal of Peasant Studies*, 41(6), 911–931.

Fold, N., & Pritchard, B. (2005). *Cross-Continental Agro-Food Chains: Structures, Actors and Dynamics in the Global Food System*. Abingdon: Routledge.

Food and Agriculture Organization of the UN (FAO). (2018). *The State of Agricultural Commodity Markets 2018: Agricultural Trade, Climate Change and Food Security*. Rome: FAO.

Food and Agriculture Organization of the UN (FAO), IFAD, UNICEF, WFP, & WHO. (2021). *The State of Food Security and Nutrition in the World 2021*. Rome: FAO.

Fouilleux, E., Bricas, N., & Alpha, A. (2017). "Feeding 9 Billion People": Global Food Security Debates and the Productionist Trap. *Journal of European Public Policy*, 24(11), 1658–1677.

Fresh Plaza. (2020). Chinese Avocado Imports Plummet by 19%. *Fresh Plaza*. August 19. www.freshplaza.com/article/9241541/chinese-avocado-imports-plummet-by-19/.

Friedmann, H. (1982). The Political Economy of Food: The Rise and Fall of the Postwar International Food Order. *American Journal of Sociology*, 88, S248–S286.

Friedmann, H. (1992). Distance and Durability: Shaky Foundations of the World Food Economy. *Third World Quarterly*, 13(2), 371–383.

Friedmann, H. (2005). From Colonialism to Green Capitalism: Social Movements and Emergence of Food Regimes. In F. H. Buttel & P. McMichael (eds.), *New Directions in the Sociology of Global Development* (pp. 227–264). Bingley: Emerald Group Publishing Limited.

Friedmann, H., & McMichael, P. (1989). Agriculture and the State System: The Rise and Decline of National Agricultures, 1870 to the Present. *Sociologia Ruralis*, 29(2), 93–117.

Friis, C., & Nielsen, J. Ø. (2016). Small-Scale Land Acquisitions, Large-Scale Implications: Exploring the Case of Chinese Banana Investments in Northern Laos. *Land Use Policy*, 57, 117–129.

Fuchs, R., Alexander, P., Brown, C. et al. (2019). Why the US–China Trade War Spells Disaster for the Amazon. *Nature*, 567, 451–454.

Gale, F., Valdes, C., & Ash, M. (2019). *Interdependence of China, United States, and Brazil in Soybean Trade, OCS-19F-01*. Washington, DC: US Department of Agriculture.

Gaudreau, M. (2019). State Food Security and People's Food Sovereignty: Competing Visions of Agriculture in China. *Canadian Journal of Development Studies/Revue canadienne d'études du développement*, 40(1), 12–28.

Goetz, A. (2015). How Different Are the UK and China? Investor Countries in Comparative Perspective. *Canadian Journal of Development Studies/Revue canadienne d'études du développement*, 36(2), 179–195.

Gong, H., Meng, D., Li, X., & Zhu, F. (2013). Soil Degradation and Food Security Coupled with Global Climate Change in Northeastern China. *Chinese Geographical Science*, 23(5), 562–573.

Gong, P. (2011). China Needs No Foreign Help to Feed Itself. *Nature News*, 474(7349), 7–7.

Gong, W., & Zhang, Q. F. (2017). Betting on the Big: State-Brokered Land Transfers, Large-Scale Agricultural Producers, and Rural Policy Implementation. *The China Journal*, 77(1), 1–26.

Gonzalez, C. G. (2002). Institutionalizing Inequality: The WTO Agreement on Agriculture, Food Security, and Developing Countries. *Columbia Journal of Environmental Law*, 27, 433–490.

Gooch, E., & Gale, F. (2018). *China's Foreign Agriculture Investments, EIB-192*. Washington, DC: US Department of Agriculture.

GRAIN. (2008). Seized: The 2008 Land Grab for Food and Financial Security. https://grain.org/article/entries/93-seized-the-2008-landgrab-for-food-and-financial-security.

Grainwiz. (2009). The Saga of China's Rising Soy Imports and Prices. May 27. www.grainwiz.com/nouvelles/797-la-saga-de-l-augmentation-de-l-importation-chinoise-de-soya-et-des-prix.

Hall, D. (2013). Primitive Accumulation, Accumulation by Dispossession and the Global Land Grab. *Third World Quarterly*, 34(9), 1582–1604.

Han, D. (2005). Why Has China's Agriculture Survived WTO Accession? *Asian Survey*, 45(6), 931–948.

Han, J. (2019). Press Conference on "Opinion on Faciliating Organic Integration between Small Farming Households and Modern Agricultural Development" (《关于促进小农户和现代农业发展有机衔接的意见》发布会). www.moa.gov.cn/hd/zbft_news/xnhxdnyfz/wzzb/.

Harvey, D. (1981). The Spatial Fix: Hegel, von Thunen, and Marx. *Antipode*, 13(3), 1–12.

Hayward, J. (2017). Beyond the Ownership Question: Who Will Till the Land? The New Debate on China's Agricultural Production. *Critical Asian Studies*, 49(4), 523–545.

He, X. (2016). Thoughts on Scaling Up Agriculture in China (关于我国农业经营规模的思考). *Issues in Agricultural Economy (Chinese)*, (9), 4–15.

Hess, S. (2015). Foreign Media Coverage and Protest Outcomes in China: The Case of the 2011 Wukan Rebellion. *Modern Asian Studies*, 49(1), 177–203.

Hofman, I. (2016). Politics or Profits along the "Silk Road": What Drives Chinese Farms in Tajikistan and Helps Them Thrive? *Eurasian Geography and Economics*, 57(3), 457–481.

Hofman, I., & Ho, P. (2012). China's "Developmental Outsourcing": A Critical Examination of Chinese Global "Land Grabs" Discourse. *Journal of Peasant Studies*, 39(1), 1–48.

Hopewell, K. (2020). *Clash of Powers: US–China Rivalry in Global Trade Governance*. Cambridge: Cambridge University Press.

Hsing, Y.-t. (2010). *The Great Urban Transformation: Politics of Land and Property in China*: Oxford: Oxford University Press.

Hu, Y., Cheng, H., & Tao, S. (2017a). Environmental and Human Health Challenges of Industrial Livestock and Poultry Farming in China and Their Mitigation. *Environment International*, 107, 111–130.

Hu, Z., Zhang, Q. F., & Donaldson, J. A. (2017b). Farmers' Cooperatives in China: A Typology of Fraud and Failure. *The China Journal*, 78(1), 1–24.

Huang, J. (2013). Food Supply: Enough for Everyone. *China Economic Quarterly*, 7(3), 20–23.

Huang, J., & Rozelle, S. (2002). *China's Accession to WTO and Shifts in the Agriculture Policy*. Working paper, University of California–Davis, Department of Agricultural and Resource Economics.

Huang, J., Wei, W., Qi, C., & Wei, X. (2017). The Prospects for China's Food Security and Imports: Will China Starve the World via Imports? *Journal of Integrative Agriculture*, 16(12), 2933–2944.

Huang, P. C. (2016). China's Hidden Agricultural Revolution, 1980–2010, in Historical and Comparative Perspective. *Modern China*, 42(4), 339–376.

Jakobsen, J. (2021). New Food Regime Geographies: Scale, State, Labor. *World Development*, 145, 105523.

Kenney-Lazar, M. (2018). Governing Dispossession: Relational Land Grabbing in Laos. *Annals of the American Association of Geographers*, 108(3), 679–694.

Kimbrell, A. (2002). *The Fatal Harvest Reader: The Tragedy of Industrial Agriculture*. Washington, DC: Island Press.

Kong, X., Zhang, X., Lal, R. et al. (2016). Groundwater Depletion by Agricultural Intensification in China's HHH Plains, since 1980s. *Advances in Agronomy*, 135, 59–106.

Krausmann, F., & Langthaler, E. (2019). Food Regimes and Their Trade Links: A Socio-ecological Perspective. *Ecological Economics*, 160, 87–95.

Kuang, W., Liu, J., Dong, J., Chi, W., & Zhang, C. (2016). The Rapid and Massive Urban and Industrial Land Expansions in China between 1990 and 2010: A CLUD-Based Analysis of Their Trajectories, Patterns, and Drivers. *Landscape and Urban Planning*, 145, 21–33.

La Via Campesina (LVC). (2007). Declaration of Nyéléni. https://nyeleni.org/IMG/pdf/DeclNyeleni-en.pdf.

Lawther, I. (2017). Why African Countries Are Interested in Building Agricultural Partnerships with China: Lessons from Rwanda and Uganda. *Third World Quarterly*, 38(10), 2312–2329.

Lee, C. K. (2016). Precarization or Empowerment? Reflections on Recent Labor Unrest in China. *The Journal of Asian Studies*, 75(2), 317–333.

Lee, C. K. (2017). *The Specter of Global China: Politics, Labor, and Foreign Investment in Africa*. Chicago: University of Chicago Press.

Lee, C. K. (2019). China's Precariats. *Globalizations*, 16(2), 137–154.

Lee, C. K., & Zhang, Y. (2013). The Power of Instability: Unraveling the Microfoundations of Bargained Authoritarianism in China. *American Journal of Sociology*, 118(6), 1475–1508.

Lee, S., & Müller, A. R. (2012). *South Korean External Strategy Qualms: Analysis of Korean Overseas Agricultural Investment within the Global Food System*. Paper presented at the International Conference on Global Land Grabbing II (October 17–19), Cornell University, Ithaca, NY.

Li, Z. (2021). Ministry of Agriculture and Rural Affairs: Accelerate the Implementation of Regulations on Transfer of Rural Land Operation Rights (农业农村部: 加快制定农村土地经营权流转管理办法实施细则). *Jingji Cankaobao*. September 14.

Liang, W. (2002). China's WTO Negotiation Process and Its Implications. *Journal of Contemporary China*, 11(33), 683–719.

Liu, W., Yang, H., Ciais, P., Kummu, M., & Hoekstra, A. Y. (2020). China's Food Supply Sources under Trade Conflict with the United States and Limited Domestic Land and Water Resources. *Earth's Future*, 8(3), e2020EF001482.

Lu, J. (2020). Agricultural Investment of Chinese Enterprises in Russia against the Backgroup of the BRI: Features, Changes and Problems (一带一路"背景下中国企业对俄罗斯农业投资的特点、变化及问题). *Practice in Foreign Economic Relations and Trade*, 27(7), 85–92.

Lu, J., & Schönweger, O. (2019). Great Expectations: Chinese Investment in Laos and the Myth of Empty Land. *Territory, Politics, Governance*, 7(1), 61–78.

Lu, Y., Bai, Y., & Luo, G. (2020). In Depth: Three Years after Record-Breaking Syngenta Acquisition, ChemChina Struggling under Debt Mountain. *Caixin Global*. July 23.

Luo, Q., Andreas, J., & Li, Y. (2017). Grapes of Wrath: Twisting Arms to Get Villagers to Cooperate with Agribusiness in China. *The China Journal*, 77(1), 27–50.

Magnan, A. (2012). Food Regimes. In J. M. Pilcher (ed.), *The Oxford Handbook of Food History* (pp. 370–388). Oxford: Oxford University Press.

Martindale, L. (2021). From Land Consolidation and Food Safety to Taobao Villages and Alternative Food Networks: Four Components of China's Dynamic Agri-Rural Innovation System. *Journal of Rural Studies*, 82, 404–416.

Mason-D'Croz, D., Bogard, J. R., Herrero, M. et al. (2020). Modelling the Global Economic Consequences of a Major African Swine Fever Outbreak in China. *Nature Food*, 1(4), 221–228.

McClintock, N. (2010). Why Farm the City? Theorizing Urban Agriculture through a Lens of Metabolic Rift. *Cambridge Journal of Regions, Economy and Society*, 3(2), 191–207.

McKay, B. M., & Veltmeyer, H. (2021). Industrial Agriculture and Agrarian Extractivism. In *Handbook of Critical Agrarian Studies* (pp. 503–514). Cheltenham: Edward Elgar Publishing.

McKeon, N. (2021). Global Food Governance. *Development*, 64(3), 172–180.

McMichael, P. (2000). A global interpretation of the rise of the East Asian food import complex. *World Development*, 28(3), 409–424.

McMichael, P. (2005). Global Development and the Corporate Food Regime. In F. H. Buttel & P. McMichael (eds.), *Research in Rural Sociology and Development* (pp. 265–299). Bingley: Emerald Group Publishing Limited.

McMichael, P. (2009). A Food Regime Genealogy. *Journal of Peasant Studies*, 36(1), 139–169.

McMichael, P. (2012). The Land Grab and Corporate Food Regime Restructuring. *Journal of Peasant Studies*, 39(3–4), 681–701.

McMichael, P. (2013). Land Grabbing as Security Mercantilism in International Relations. *Globalizations*, 10(1), 47–64.

McMichael, P. (2020). Does China's "Going Out" Strategy Prefigure a New Food Regime? *Journal of Peasant Studies*, 47(1), 116–154.

Ministry of Agriculture and Rural Affairs (MOARA). (2019). *Report on China's Agricultural Outward Investment and Cooperation 2019 (*中国农业对外投资合作分析报告 *2019)*. Beijing: China Agriculture Press.

Ministry of Agriculture and Rural Affairs (MOARA). (2020a). China's agricultural imports and exports in 2019 (2019年我国农产品进出口情况). www.moa.gov.cn/ztzl/nybrl/rlxx/202002/t20200218_6337263.htm.

Ministry of Agriculture and Rural Affairs (MOARA). (2020b). Large companies are the major force of international agricultural cooperation (大型企业是国际农业合作的主要力量). www.fecc.agri.cn/yjzx/yjzx_yjcg/202009/t20200907_360576.html.

Ministry of Agriculture and Rural Affairs (MOARA). (2021). The List of Top 100 Dragonhead Companies and Top 10 Specialized Dragonhead Companies in 2020 Released (2020年农业产业化龙头企业100强和专项10强名单发布). www.xccys.moa.gov.cn/nycyh/202104/t20210426_6366634.htm.

Ministry of Agriculture of China (MOA). (2009). *Statistical Data of Agriculture of China in 60 years (*新中国农业60年统计资料*)*. Beijing: China Agricultural Press.

Ministry of Agriculture of China (MOA). 2017. *Vision and Action on Jointly Promoting Agricultural Cooperation on the Belt and Road.* http://english.scio.gov.cn/beltandroad/2017-05/13/content_76329324.htm.

Montenegro de Wit, M., Canfield, M., Iles, A. et al. (2021). Resetting power in global food governance: The UN Food Systems Summit. *Development*, 64(3), 153–161.

Mora, S. (2022). Land Grabbing, Power Configurations and Trajectories of China's Investments in Argentina. *Globalizations*, 19(5), 696–710.

Morton, K. (2012). *Learning By Doing: China's Role in the Global Governance of Food Security.* Working paper 30, Indiana University Research Center for Chinese Politics & Business.

Mullen, A. (2021. China Inflation: Consumer Price Growth Accelerates Due to Rising Food Costs. *The South China Morning Post*. December 9.

Myers, M., & Guo J. (2015). China's Agricultural Investment in Latin America: A Critical Assessment. *The Dialogue.* www.thedialogue.org/wp-content/uploads/2015/06/Chinas-Agricultural-Investment-in-Latin-America.pdf.

Nally, D. (2015). Governing Precarious Lives: Land Grabs, Geopolitics, and "Food Security." *The Geographical Journal*, 181(4), 340–349.

Nanfang Daily. (2013). Cadmium-Rice Crisis Sounds the Alarm of Soil Pollution ("镉米危机"敲响土壤污染警钟). *Nanfang Daily*, June 13.

National Bureau of Statistics (NBS). (1991). *China Statistical Yearbook 1991.* Beijing: China Statistics Press.

National Bureau of Statistics (NBS). (1999). *Comprehensive Statistical Data and Materials on 50 Years of New China.* Beijing: China Statistics Press.

National Bureau of Statistics (NBS). (2009). *China Compendium of Statistics 1949–2008.* Beijing: China Statistics Press.

National Bureau of Statistics (NBS). (2020). *China Statistical Yearbook 2020.* Beijing: China Statistics Press.

National Bureau of Statistics (NBS). (2021a). National Database. https://data .stats.gov.cn/.

National Bureau of Statistics (NBS). (2021b). The No. 7 Report on the Seventh National Census (第七次全国人口普查公报第七号). www.stats.gov.cn/ tjsj/tjgb/rkpcgb/qgrkpcgb/202106/t20210628_1818826.html.

National Bureau of Statistics (NBS). (2021c). *Statistical Report of the People's Republic of China on the 2020 National Economic and Social Development.* Beijing: National Bureau of Statistics of China.

Niehaus, A., & Walravens, T. (2017). *Feeding Japan: The Cultural and Political Issues of Dependency and Risk.* Cham: Palgrave Macmillan.

Nolte, K., Chamberlain, W., & Giger, M. (2016). *International Land Deals for Agriculture: Fresh Insights from the Land Matrix: Analytical Report II.* Bern: Bern Open Publishing.

O'Brien, K. J., & Li, L. (2006). *Rightful Resistance in Rural China.* Cambridge: Cambridge University Press.

Observatory of Economic Complexity (OEC). (2021). Database of the Observatory of Economic Complexity. https://oec.world/en.

Oliveira, G. d. L. (2018). Chinese Land Grabs in Brazil? Sinophobia and Foreign Investments in Brazilian Soybean Agribusiness. *Globalizations*, 15(1), 114–133.

Oliveira, G. d. L., McKay, B. M., & Liu, J. (2021). Beyond land grabs: New insights on land struggles and global agrarian change. *Globalizations*, 18(3), 321–338.

Oliveira, G. d. L., & Schneider, M. (2016). The Politics of Flexing Soybeans: China, Brazil and Global Agroindustrial Restructuring. *Journal of Peasant Studies*, 43(1), 167–194.

Organisation for Economic Co-operation and Development (OECD) & FAO. (2020). *OECD–FAO Agricultural Outlook 2020–2029.* Rome: FAO.

Ouyang, H. (2011). Nearly 70% of Respondents Lack a Sense of Food Safety: Report on Consumer Confidence in food SAFETY 2010–2011 (近七成受访者对食品没有安全感: 2010–2011消费者食品安全信心报告). *Xiaokang*, (1), 42–45.

Patel, R. (2009). Food sovereignty. *Journal of Peasant Studies*, 36(3), 663–706.

Patel, R. (2012). *Stuffed and Starved: The Hidden Battle for the World Food System.* New York: Melville House.

Pawlak, K., Kołodziejczak, M., & Xie, Y. (2016). Changes in Foreign Trade in Agri-Food Products between the EU and China. *Journal of Agribusiness and Rural Development*, 42(4), 607–618.

Pechlaner, G., & Otero, G. (2008). The Third Food Regime: Neoliberal Globalism and Agricultural Biotechnology in North America. *Sociologia Ruralis*, 48(4), 351–371.

Polanyi, K. (2001 [1944]). *The Great Transformation: The Political and Economic Origins of Our Time*. Boston: Beacon Press.

Pritchard, B. (2009). The Long Hangover from the Second Food Regime: A World-Historical Interpretation of the Collapse of the WTO Doha Round. *Agriculture and Human Values*, 26(4), 297–307.

Qi, J., Zheng, X., & Guo, H. (2019). The Formation of Taobao Villages in China. *China Economic Review*, 53, 106–127.

Qiao, J. (2019). Maintain Grain Production above 650 Million Tons This Year (把全年粮食产量稳定在1.3万亿斤以上). *The Economic Daily*. August 3. www.ce.cn/cysc/sp/info/201908/03/t20190803_32800649.shtml.

Ren, T. (2019). 70 Years of COFCO as a Trailblazer (中粮七十年, 敢为天下先). *Guozi Baogao (*国资报告*)*, (12), 84–88.

Rowley, L. (2020). Boom and Bust: Is China Bowing Out of Australian Agriculture? www.beefcentral.com/property/boom-and-bust-is-china-bowing-out-of-australian-agriculture/.

Sargeson, S. (2013). Violence as Development: Land Expropriation and China's Urbanization. *Journal of Peasant Studies*, 40(6), 1063–1085.

Schmalzer, S. (2016). *Red Revolution, Green Revolution: Scientific Farming in Socialist China*. Chicago: University of Chicago Press.

Schneider, M. (2015). What, Then, Is a Chinese Peasant? Nongmin Discourses and Agroindustrialization in Contemporary China. *Agriculture and Human Values*, 32(2), 331–346.

Schneider, M. (2017). Dragon Head Enterprises and the State of Agribusiness in China. *Journal of Agrarian Change*, 17(1), 3–21.

Scott, S., Si, Z., Schumilas, T., & Chen, A. (2018). *Organic Food and Farming in China: Top-Down and Bottom-Up Ecological Initiatives*. Abingdon: Routledge.

Shiva, V. (2001). *Stolen Harvest: The Hijacking of the Global Food Supply*. London: Zed Books.

Si, Z., Li, Y., Fang, P., & Zhou, L. (2019). "One Family, Two Systems": Food Safety Crisis as a Catalyst for Agrarian Changes in Rural China. *Journal of Rural Studies*, 69, 87–96.

Si, Z., Schumilas, T., & Scott, S. (2015). Characterizing Alternative Food Networks in China. *Agriculture and Human Values*, 32(2), 299–313.

Si, Z., & Scott, S. (2016). The Convergence of Alternative Food Networks within "Rural Development" Initiatives: The Case of the New Rural Reconstruction Movement in China. *Local Environment*, 21(9), 1082–1099.

Sina. (2016). Beidahuang Left a Mess in Its Endeavour to Join Fortune 500, with the Former Director in Prison (北大荒冲世界500强留下一地鸡毛 前任掌门人锒铛入狱). December 22. http://finance.sina.com.cn/chanjing/gsnews/2016-12-22/doc-ifxyxury7967600.shtml.

So, A. Y., & Chu, Y.-w. (2016). *The Global Rise of China*. Cambridge: Polity Press.

Søndergaard, N. (2020). Repercussions of Chinese Land Deals in South America: Vectors of Mobilization and Domestic Institutions. *Revista de Sociologia e Política*, 28(74), e007.

Tang, K., Wang, J., & Chen, Z. (2017). The Impact of Farm Size of Rural Households on Grain Output and Production Costs (农户耕地经营规模对粮食单产和生产成本的影响). *Journal of Management World (Chinese)*, (5), 79–91.

The State Council. (2008). Outline of the Medium- and Long-Term Plan for National Food Security (2008–2020). www.gov.cn/jrzg/2008-11/13/content_1148414.htm.

The State Council. (2019). White Paper: Food Security in China. http://english.scio.gov.cn/2019-10/14/content_75300394.htm.

Tortajada, C., & Zhang, H. (2021). When Food Meets BRI: China's Emerging Food Silk Road. *Global Food Security*, 29, 100518.

Trappel, R. (2015). *China's Agrarian Transition: Peasants, Property, and Politics*. London: Lexington Books.

UN. (2015). All food systems are sustainable. www.un.org/en/issues/food/taskforce/pdf/All%20food%20systems%20are%20sustainable.pdf.

USDA. (2020). China: Evolving demand in the world's largest agricultural import market. www.fas.usda.gov/data/china-evolving-demand-world-s-largest-agricultural-import-market.

van der Ploeg, J. D., Jingzhong, Y., & Schneider, S. (2012). Rural Development through the Construction of New, Nested, Markets: Comparative Perspectives from China, Brazil and the European Union. *Journal of Peasant Studies*, 39(1), 133–173.

Veltmeyer, H. (2013). The Political Economy of Natural Resource Extraction: A New Model or Extractive Imperialism? *Canadian Journal of Development Studies/Revue canadienne d'études du développement*, 34(1), 79–95.

Vicol, M., & Pritchard, B. (2021). Rethinking Rural Development in Myanmar's Ayeyarwady Delta through a Historical Food Regimes Frame. *Singapore Journal of Tropical Geography*, 42(2), 264–283.

Wang, K. (2018). COFCO: Meet Market Demands with a Global Vision (中粮集团: 立足全球视野满足市场需求). *The People's Daily*. July 11.

Wang, S. (2013). The Story of Soybeans: How Capital Endangers Human Security (大豆的故事: 资本如何危及人类安全). *Open Times*, 249, 87–108.

Weis, T. (2013). The Meat of the Global Food Crisis. *Journal of Peasant Studies*, 40(1), 65–85.

Wen, T. (2001). Centenary Reflections on the "Three Dimensional Problem" of Rural China. *Inter-Asia Cultural Studies*, 2(2), 287–295.

Wen, T. (2012). *Eight Crises: Lessons from China 1949–2009 (*八次危机*)*. Beijing: Dongfang chubanshe.

Woodhouse, P. (2010). Beyond Industrial Agriculture? Some Questions about Farm Size, Productivity and Sustainability. *Journal of Agrarian Change*, 10(3), 437–453.

World Bank. (2021). World Bank open data. https://data.worldbank.org/.

World Trade Organization (WTO). (2022). Domestic support in agriculture: The boxes. www.wto.org/english/tratop_e/agric_e/agboxes_e.htm.

Wu, S., & Liu, C. (2020). Further on the Issues of Grain Security in Scaled-Up Agriculture: Debates and Policy Implications (再议规模经营中的粮食安全问题: 争议回应与政策启示). *Journal of Northwest A&F University (Social Science Edition)*, 20(6), 80–87.

Wu, X., Yang, D. L., & Chen, L. (2017). The Politics of Quality-of-Life Issues: Food Safety and Political Trust in China. *Journal of Contemporary China*, 26 (106), 601–615.

Wu, Y., & Chen, Y. (2013). Food Safety in China. *Journal of Epidemiology & Community Health*, 67(6), 478–479.

Xinhua. (1998). Decision of the CCCPC on Major Issues Concerning Agriculture and Rural Areas. http://cn.chinagate.cn/indepths/zggcd90n/2011-04/13/content_22350169.htm.

Xinhua. (2018a). The Directives on Implementing the Strategy of Rural Revitalization. www.gov.cn/zhengce/2018-02/04/content_5263807.htm.

Xinhua. (2018b). COFCO's 2017 Performance Report Is Released (中粮集团2017年成绩单出炉). www.xinhuanet.com/food/2018-01/17/c_112227 2529.htm.

Xu, Z., Li, B., & Wang, Y. (2014). The Impact of the "Whole Supply Chain" Strategy on Enterprise Performance: The Case of COFCO (论"全产业链"战略对企业绩效的影响——以中粮集团为例). *Shangye Shidai (*商业时代*)*, (9), 14–17.

Yan, H., & Chen, Y. (2013). Debating the Rural Cooperative Movement in China, the Past and the Present. *Journal of Peasant Studies*, 40(6), 955–981.

Yan, H., Ku, H. B., & Xu, S. (2021). Rural Revitalization, Scholars, and the Dynamics of the Collective Future in China. *Journal of Peasant Studies*, 48(4), 853–874.

Yan, H., & Sautman, B. (2010). Chinese Farms in Zambia: From Socialist to "Agro-Imperialist" Engagement? *African and Asian studies*, 9(3), 307–333.

Yan, Y. (2012). Food Safety and Social Risk in Contemporary China. *The Journal of Asian Studies*, 71(3), 705–729.

Yang, H., Vernooy, R., & Leeuwis, C. (2018). Farmer Cooperatives and the Changing Agri-Food System in China. *China Information*, 32(3), 423–442.

Ye, J. (2015). Land Transfer and the Pursuit of Agricultural Modernization in China. *Journal of Agrarian Change*, 15(3), 314–337.

Ye, J., & He, C. (2020). Poverty Alleviation Practice and Theoretical Exploration Based on Small-Farm Household Production: A Case Study of a Small-Farm "Nested Market" Poverty Alleviation Trial. *Social Sciences in China*, 41(3), 152–172.

Zang, Y. (2013). *The Truth about Chinese Agriculture (*中国农业真相*)*. Beijing: Peking University Press.

Zhan, S. (2017a). Riding on Self-Sufficiency: Grain Policy and the Rise of Agrarian Capital in China. *Journal of Rural Studies*, 54, 151–161.

Zhan, S. (2017b). *Hukou* Reform and Land Politics in China: Rise of a Tripartite Alliance. *The China Journal*, 78(1), 25–49.

Zhan, S. (2019a). *The Land Question in China: Agrarian Capitalism, Industrious Revolution, and East Asian Development*. Abingdon: Routledge.

Zhan, S. (2019b). Accumulation by and without Dispossession: Rural Land Use, Land Expropriation, and Livelihood Implications in China. *Journal of Agrarian Change*, 19(3), 447–464.

Zhan, S. (2020a). The Land Question in 21st Century China: Four Camps and Five Scenarios. *New Left Review*, 122, 115–133.

Zhan, S. (2020b). COVID-19, Land, and Rural Struggles of the Chinese Working Class. https://marxistsociology.org/2020/09/covid-19-land-and-rural-struggles-of-the-chinese-working-class/.

Zhan, S. (2021). The Political Economy of Food Import and Self-Reliance in China: 1949–2019. *Global Food History*, 1–19. https://doi.org/10.1080/20549547.2021.2012082.

Zhan, S., & Huang, L. (2017). Internal Spatial Fix: China's Geographical Solution to Food Supply and Its Limits. *Geoforum*, 85, 140–152.

Zhan, S., & Scully, B. (2018). From South Africa to China: Land, Migrant Labor and the Semi-Proletarian Thesis Revisited. *Journal of Peasant Studies*, 45(5–6), 1018–1038.

Zhan, S., Zhang, H., & He, D. (2018). China's Flexible Overseas Food Strategy: Food Trade and Agricultural Investment between Southeast Asia and China in 1990–2015. *Globalizations*, 15(5), 702–721.

Zhang, H. (2018). *Securing the "Rice Bowl": China and Global Food Security*. Singapore: Springer.

Zhang, H. (2020). The US–China trade war: Is food China's most powerful weapon? *Asia Policy*, 27(3), 59–86.

Zhang, L. (2021). China and the UN Food System Summit: Silenced disputes and ambivalence on food safety, sovereignty, justice, and resilience. *Development*, 64(3), 303–307.

Zhang, Q. F., & Donaldson, J. A. (2008). The Rise of Agrarian Capitalism with Chinese Characteristics: Agricultural Modernization, Agribusiness and Collective Land Rights. *The China Journal,* (60), 25–47.

Zhang, Y. (2011). Migrant Workers' Willingness of Urban *Hukou* Registration and Policy Choices on Urbanization in China (农民工"进城落户"意愿与中国近期城镇化道路的选择). *Chinese Journal of Population Science,* (2), 14–26.

Zhou, J. (2016). Chinese Agrarian Capitalism in the Russian Far East. *Third World Thematics: A TWQ Journal*, 1(5), 612–632.

Zou, L., Liu, Y., Wang, Y., & Hu, X. (2020). Assessment and Analysis of Agricultural Non-point Source Pollution Loads in China: 1978–2017. *Journal of Environmental Management*, 263, 110400.

Cambridge Elements

Global China

Ching Kwan Lee
University of California–Los Angeles

Ching Kwan Lee is professor of sociology at the University of California–Los Angeles. Her scholarly interests include political sociology, popular protests, labor, development, political economy, comparative ethnography, China, Hong Kong, East Asia and the Global South. She is the author of three multiple award-winning monographs on contemporary China: Gender and the South China Miracle: Two Worlds of Factory Women (1998), Against the Law: Labor Protests in China's Rustbelt and Sunbelt (2007), and The Specter of Global China: Politics, Labor and Foreign Investment in Africa (2017). Her co-edited volumes include Take Back Our Future: an Eventful Sociology of Hong Kong's Umbrella Movement (2019) and The Social Question in the 21st Century: A Global View (2019).

About the Series

The Cambridge Elements series Global China showcases thematic, region- or country-specific studies on China's multifaceted global engagements and impacts. Each title, written by a leading scholar of the subject matter at hand, combines a succinct, comprehensive and up-to-date overview of the debates in the scholarly literature with original analysis and a clear argument. Featuring cutting edge scholarship on arguably one of the most important and controversial developments in the 21st century, the Global China Elements series will advance a new direction of China scholarship that expands China Studies beyond China's territorial boundaries.

Cambridge Elements ☰

Global China

Printed in the United States
by Baker & Taylor Publisher Services